AMERICAN JUDAISM

American

THE CHICAGO HISTORY OF AMERICAN CIVILIZATION

Daniel J. Boorstin, EDITOR

Judaism

By Nathan Glazer
Second Edition

THE UNIVERSITY OF CHICAGO PRESS
CHICAGO AND LONDON

THE UNIVERSITY OF CHICAGO PRESS, CHICAGO 60637

The University of Chicago Press, Ltd., London

© 1957, 1972 by The University of Chicago. All rights
reserved. Published 1957. Second Edition 1972
Printed in The United States of America

86 85 84 83 82 81 80 79 76543

ISBN: 0–226–29839–6 (clothbound); 0–226-29841–8 (paperbound)
Library of Congress Catalog Card Number: 72–85433

To My Father

LOUIS GLAZER

Editor's Preface to the Second Edition

Any book on religion in America makes large demands of its author. The historian of Judaism in particular faces special problems. Unlike Catholicism, with its hierarchy and an authenticated creed, or the Protestant sects, with their distinctive theological traditions, Judaism is somehow a "people-religion." An American rabbi has described the American Jewish community as a people in quest of a definition. While other American religions provide the historian with a reasonably clear definition of what he must discuss, the historian of Judaism, especially if he is himself a Jew, must try to find in his history a better definition of what it is that he is writing about.

Mr. Glazer here makes a virtue of this difficulty. His interpretation of Judaism as the quest for a holy community leads him to scrutinize those American circumstances which have affected the character of all community life in the New World, from the earliest problems of the new immigrant to the latest problems of suburbia. He has not ignored those strong pressures within American culture which have led all the major American religions to grow more like one another. But he does not always rejoice at this assimilation. He asks whether in this process American life may not have lost something, and he asks whether a bland national religion can be vital, or indeed truly religious at all.

Needless to say, Mr. Glazer's interpretation will not please all Jews, or even all the members of any particular branch of American Judaism. This is in part, of course, because he writes from

Editor's Preface to the Second Edition

within the Jewish tradition, where, in the absence of authorized theology, the tasks of interpretation are thrust back upon the individual.

In telling the story of a people with a vivid tradition who have had to come to terms with the New World, Mr. Glazer is retelling the story of all Americans. He helps us understand how many ancient, iridescent threads have been woven into the complex fabric of American culture, producing a still more remarkable iridescence.

In seeing his subject as an illustration of the broadest problems of American history, Mr. Glazer admirably serves the purpose of the "Chicago History of American Civilization," which aims to make each aspect of our culture a window to all our history. The series contains two kinds of books: a *chronological* group, which will provide a coherent narrative of American history from its beginning to the present day, and a *topical* group, which will deal with the history of varied and significant aspects of American life. This book is one of the topical group.

In this second edition Mr. Glazer has made numerous revisions throughout the text and added an important additional chapter. He brings his interpretation up to date and helps the reader relate the story of recent American Judaism to the new currents stirring in American life.

DANIEL J. BOORSTIN

Acknowledgments

This book was made possible by two foundations: the John Simon Guggenheim Memorial Foundation, which granted me a fellowship in 1954 for research on the sociology of American Jews, and the Walgreen Foundation of the University of Chicago, which invited me to deliver a series of lectures on American Judaism—on which this book is based—in the spring of 1955. I am deeply grateful to both.

I wish to record a debt of a different sort to Elliot E. Cohen and *Commentary* magazine, which he created and on which I worked from 1945 to 1954. *Commentary* magazine gave me an unrivaled opportunity to study, informally but continuously, the life of American Jews. Elliot Cohen was himself the best possible guide to this life: not always right, he was, what is more important than being right, almost always aware of what was significant and what was interesting.

Many people in American Jewish religious life have helped me by granting me interviews and giving me written materials. I cannot mention all of them, but I am particularly grateful to Professor Jacob Rader Marcus of Hebrew Union College, Professor Judah Goldin of the Jewish Theological Seminary of America, and Rabbi Arthur Hertzberg, formerly of Nashville, Tennessee, and now of Englewood, New Jersey. Professor Marcus told me of much interesting material, which I did not know existed, and then read the lectures on which this book is based, saving me from many errors. He is the most generous of scholars. Professor Goldin gave the

Acknowledgments

benefit of his experience as a rabbi, teacher, and scholar and arranged for me to visit classes at the Jewish Theological Seminary. Rabbi Hertzberg, one of the most scholarly and thoughtful of rabbis, made it possible for me to visit Nashville and served as my guide to the Jewish community there. My friends Milton Himmelfarb, Jacob Taubes, and Daniel Bell read some or all of the original lectures critically; I am grateful for their comments. Moshe Davis and Jacob Neusner read the final manuscript; I am indebted to them for their comments. An editor myself, I was able to appreciate the careful and sympathetic reading of this book by Daniel J. Boorstin, editor of the series in which it appears; he has helped to improve it greatly.

I wish to thank Doubleday and Company for so generously giving me a leave, only a little while after I came to work for them, so that I could accept the Guggenheim Foundation fellowship.

For the second edition of this book, relatively few changes have been made in the text of the first edition, except where there was better information. A new chapter has been added, chapter ix, covering developments from 1956 to 1972. I have made additions to the sections "Important Dates" and "Suggested Reading." I prepared the second edition of this book at the Center for Advanced Study in the Behavioral Sciences, in Stanford, California, where I was a Fellow during the academic year 1971–72, and I wish to express my gratitude to the Center for offering me a free year for scholarly pursuits.

Nathan Glazer

Contents

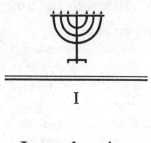

I

Introduction

The American people are generally divided into three major religious groups: Protestants, Catholics, and Jews. Like all convenient divisions, this one coincides only approximately with reality. Important groups such as the adherents of the Eastern Orthodox churches fit easily into none of these categories. Moreover, the three groups differ greatly in strength and character, and to call them all "religions" is to obscure important distinctions among them.

Despite these difficulties, the division has taken hold, and one may expect nowadays to see rabbis, as well as ministers and priests, open sessions of political conventions and bless the deliberations of Congress. It would be an interesting essay in the history of ideas to determine just how the United States evolved in the popular mind from a "Christian" nation into a nation made up of Catholics, Protestants, and Jews. The most interesting part of such a study— which I do not plan to undertake here—would be to discover how it came about that the Jewish group, which through most of the history of the United States has formed an insignificant percentage of the American people, has come to be granted the status of a "most favored religion."

Certainly the impressive history of the Jews has played some role in giving them this position. Their numbers in America scarcely justify it. Jews at present make up about 3 per cent of the population of the United States, and this small percentage reflects the migration of Jews that took place between fifty and ninety years ago. Before the 1880's, Jews formed only a fraction of 1 per cent of the American people. There are today probably about six million Jews in the United States.

Since the United States government does not inquire about religious affiliation in its decennial censuses, the number of Jews in this country is arrived at by a series of educated and highly sophisticated guesses. Nevertheless, these guesses can be taken as not far from the fact. They are based on estimates made by local Jewish communities by various means: from miniature censuses to estimates based on the number of children absent from school on major Jewish holidays. It is the last method that is often used in the largest Jewish communities, in New York City for example. In 1957, for the first and only time, the United States Bureau of the Census asked a national sample of the American population a question on its religion. This was not in the regular decennial census but in one of the Census Bureau's Current Population Surveys. This has been an invaluable source of data on the Jewish population, and it reassured Jewish demographers that the estimates they had made by cruder means were not very far off.[1]

Decennial censuses of religion have been conducted under government auspices (the last was in 1936), but these are conducted by the denominations themselves and are principally useful for giving us the number of church buildings, their money value, and similar facts. The number of members of each denomination is a figure largely determined by the theologically oriented definition of each group, and it is hazardous to use these figures. Thus, in 1936, every Jew in a community in which there was a congregation was considered a member of the Jewish denomination. This generous definition in effect meant that the

number of Jews as given in the religious census was just about
the number of Jews in the country; no distinction was made between Jews who were members of synagogues and Jews who
were not. The Catholic definition of a church member approaches this Jewish one in comprehensiveness. Many Protestant denominations tend to limit members to adults and adolescents who specifically identify themselves with a church.
For this reason, if one adds up the number of Jews, Catholics,
and Protestants as given in lists of members of American religions (for example, in the *Yearbook of American Churches*),
these differences of definition will be reflected, and Jews will
form $4\frac{1}{2}$ per cent of all church members, and Catholics 37 per
cent. Actually these are considerably inflated figures for both
groups.

Aside from their relatively small numbers, the Jews diverge in
other respects from the major religious groups in the United States.
These divergences are the result of the original character of their
religion, the particular history of the Jews before they arrived in
America, and the nature of American society at the time of the
major Jewish migrations to this country. Many of these divergences
will emerge in the course of the present study. But there is one distinction between the Jews and the other major American religious
groups that is so significant that we must consider it at the outset.
As against the Christian churches—and even the non-Christian
religions like Islam and Buddhism, which have some adherents in
the United States—Judaism is tied up organically with a specific
people, indeed, a nation.* The tie is so intimate that the word
"Jew" in common usage refers ambiguously both to an adherent
of the religion of Judaism and to a member of the Jewish people.

* I use the word nation to refer to a group of people who feel they have a
common identity and a common cultural heritage, who may feel they are of
common descent, who may speak a common language, who may inhabit a
contiguous stretch of territory, and who may on occasion form a nation-state.

American Judaism

The two categories are logically distinct, as is demonstrated by the existence of Jewish Christians (i.e., individuals of the Jewish nation and the Christian religion) in the early centuries of the Christian Era, and the Roman Jews (i.e., individuals of the Roman nation and the Jewish religion) of the same period. And today, too, one can find people who consider themselves Jews by religion and who are members of other national groups, as well as people who consider themselves Jews by race and who are adherents of other religions. In countries where the census asks not only for religion but for ethnic* identification—as in Canada, and in Czechoslovakia between the wars—one can find a few individuals who belong to these odd categories. But despite this logical distinctness between Jews by race and Jews by religion, the two form, in history and in present-day actuality, a single entity, a nation-religion.

On the American scene, one might think, this is not so decisive a distinguishing characteristic as it would be in a more ethnically homogeneous country; for here in the United States there is a certain degree of coincidence between ethnic origin and religion. While many ethnic groups are divided among a number of religions, and many religions encompass a number of ethnic groups, there does tend to be a rough correlation between ethnic group and religion, and in some cases the coincidence is almost complete or

---

This usage is familiar to students of nationalism. "Nationality," "national group," "people," and "race" all have somewhat different connotations, but all of them have been used to refer to the same social reality.

* The term "ethnic group" refers to an element in a population that feels itself, to some extent, part of a single nationality, nation, people, or race. In the United States, the Irish, Italians, and Poles, the French Canadians, Puerto Ricans, and Mexicans, the Negroes and the Jews, are thus all ethnic groups. So too were the Germans in Czechoslovakia, the Hungarians in Rumania, the Boers in South Africa. An ethnic group may be a nation, or it may be only a fragment of a nation with slight ties to the main part, as is the case with most ethnic groups in the United States.

4

Introduction

exclusive. For example, there are Lutheran and Eastern Orthodox churches which minister to the immigrants (and their descendants) coming from a single national group; we may find special Lutheran churches for Norwegians, Swedes, Danes, Finns, Slovaks, Icelanders, and others, and special Eastern Orthodox churches for Serbs, Rumanians, Bulgarians, Russians, Albanians, Czechs, and others. In what way, then, are the Jews especially to be distinguished?

In this: The ethnic element of their religion is essential to the Jews, while there is no essential relation between being a Norwegian and being a member of a Norwegian Lutheran church, or a Serbian and a member of a Serbian Orthodox church. If there happens to be no Norwegian or Serbian church in the neighborhood, one can go to another Lutheran or Eastern Orthodox church without any religious problem being raised.

In the ethnic churches, a universal religion is preached in a particular tongue. The minister or priest, it is true, often mixes up the maintenance of the ethnic group which forms his congregation with the maintenance of the religion and denounces the abandonment of the Old World tongue and customs as if this were the abandonment of the ancestral faith. In general, however, the ethnic churches in America must and do reconcile themselves to the prospect of ultimate extinction. In time, the pastor's use of a foreign language arouses more and more opposition. If the adherents of the church are concentrated in one section of the country and if they are isolated, for one reason or another, from other Americans, the old forms may be maintained for a number of generations. But, inevitably, there comes a time when the younger generation insists on English or, worse, joins a church of similar character and higher status. The adherents of the ethnic church eventually become part of one of the large American denominations. This is an inevitable by-product of the assimilation of ethnic groups in America.

In this process, no basic religious values are threatened. It is a matter of indifference to Lutheranism as a religion whether its doctrines are propagated in Norwegian, German, or English. One should not, of course, underestimate the feeling of estrangement and alienation produced in the older generation as the Americanized version of the religion spreads. But no serious thinker can contend that any threat to the religion is thereby involved. There is generally an older, fully Americanized church which maintains the same theology and polity as the declining ethnic church. The disappearance of Norwegian Lutheranism does not affect the position of Lutheranism as such.

The position of the Jews is entirely different. The addition of ethnic elements to Calvinism or Lutheranism or Roman Catholicism is fortuitous; the combination of ethnic elements with Judaism is essential. The point is almost too obvious for elaboration. Everyone knows that the Holy Scriptures of the Jewish people—what Christians know as the Old Testament—is the history of the Jews. A large part of the Jewish religion consists of ceremonies that celebrate and recall this national history. A good part of the rest consists of the customs of the Jewish people, once the cultural traits of a specific people but now become holy and incorporated into the religious code of law which is fundamental to Judaism. Judaism refers to an enormous body of practices, embracing one's entire life, more than it refers to a body of doctrine.

With such a character, it is inconceivable that Judaism could survive the disappearance of the Jewish people, except as a subject for scholarly study. And so the assimilation of Jews—that is, the disappearance of Jews as an identifiable and distinct people—is a real threat to the Jewish religion. Indeed, even the loss of specific ethnic characteristics short of complete assimilation (the process we may call acculturation), which to every other religion in

Introduction

America is—or should be—a matter of indifference, is of fundamental importance for the Jewish religion. Judaism is, in large measure, a historical creation of the way Jews have lived; while the way Jews have lived, and the way they live today, is, in large measure, a creation of Judaism. It seems impossible to divide the two.

Efforts have been made to do so. In the late nineteenth and early twentieth centuries, under the influence of new tendencies in politics and religion, there were determined attempts to dissolve this relationship between the Jewish people and the Jewish religion. Jewish nationalists—Zionists and others, though not all of them—sought to dispense with the Jewish religion and make the Jewish nation like all other nations, one in which religion would be a matter of taste. Somewhat earlier, Jewish religious reformers tried to dispense with all the national elements in the Jewish religion and make it like other religions, indifferent to the fate and character of a single people. Both efforts, one may now safely say, failed. The antireligious tendencies of Zionism and the antinational tendencies of Reform Judaism have become muted. It tells us something about the nature of the Jewish religion that Reform, the most consciously rational and universalizing Jewish religious tendency, now incorporates in its educational practices Jewish folk customs which have no religious significance but which are nevertheless recognized as being essential to the continuance of Judaism.

At an earlier stage of human history, this close link between nation and religion was universal. The religions of the Egyptians, the Greeks, and the Romans made no clear distinctions between the two concepts. But today in America Judaism stands out as unique. In a world in which religion tends to be increasingly divorced from nationality, Judaism maintains the connection in so profound and organic a form that it makes the idea of a divorce incredible.

And since these two elements are always present, it is always possible for religious leaders and laymen to move in one or the other direction: toward the idea of a nation or a people, or toward the idea of a religion. At times, emphasis has been placed on the notion of a "pure" religion, divorced from peculiar national characteristics; at other times, the emphasis on the national character_istics, on the Jewish people, has become so strong within parts of American Judaism that it has obscured what seem to a modern mind the properly religious elements in Judaism—the relation to God, the idea of salvation, and the like.

A good part of this book will describe and analyze the movement in the United States between these two polar conceptions of the Jewish religion.

But there are other consequences of this distinctiveness of Judaism for American Jews. Judaism, we have pointed out, must resist the assimilation of American Jews. There are different branches of Judaism in America today, and they take somewhat different attitudes to assimilation, but even the most liberal interpretation of Judaism must fight the assimilation of Jews. Inevitably this leads to a certain embarrassment among American Jews—an embarrassment, I must hasten to add, that is today more potential than actual but that, our analysis of the nature of the Jewish religion must convince us, will always exist. In the United States—and indeed in most modern states—the Jews live in a society that expects to see their ethnic particularity ultimately abandoned. There has been much talk of the possibility of "cultural pluralism" in America, that is, of a state of affairs in which each ethnic group maintains, in large measure, a separate way of life, with its own customs, its own supplementary schools, its special organizations and periodicals, and perhaps even its favored secondary languages. This possibility will be discussed at greater length in chapter vi. For the moment, it is enough to say that most American ethnic groups do not seem to be moving in that direction and that the tendency of the modern state is to favor a high degree of homogeneity in its population. Where ethnic difference is of no great significance—as in the Soviet Union, after the ruthless destruction of independent leadership groups among the ethnic minorities, or in the United States, where most of the ethnic groups desire to become assimilated—then the state may look benignly upon the maintenance of folk customs and even encourage them. Where differences, however, are great, then the modern state does find it necessary to take measures to reduce them—as in the drive to Americanize the immigrants.

Indeed, Jews have been prominent in the fight to forward the assimilation of ethnic groups—to a certain extent. What is the effect of opening up occupational opportunities, educational opportunities, and residential areas to all groups but to forward their assimilation? Those religious groups most fearful of assimilation, knowing this well, limit themselves to a narrow range of occupations, do not send their children to public schools, live close together in a small area. Even among Jews this pattern is followed by extremely Orthodox groups. Most Jewish leaders press for the opening of all possible areas to Jews and other peoples, but they soon become aware of a limit beyond which Jews themselves will not press. There comes a time—and it is just about upon us—when American Jews become aware of a contradiction between the kind of society America wants to become—and indeed the kind of society most Jews want it to be—and the demands of the Jewish religion. This religion, after all, prohibits intermarriage, asserts that the Jews are a people apart, and insists that they consider themselves in exile until God restores them to the Land of Israel.* The

* Reform Jews do not consider themselves in exile; they do disapprove of intermarriage.

sociologist may intervene to ask whether these purely theological doctrines significantly affect Jewish behavior. We must answer that, as a matter of fact, despite their strong desire for integration into American society, Jews do not, on the whole, intermarry and do maintain themselves apart. How to resolve this contradiction is one of the major dilemmas of Judaism in America.

Judaism, as I have described it, is not at home in the modern world. Its difficulties, however, should be seen in context, for religion in general is not at home in the modern world. The problems of Judaism in part stem from the fact that it remains a nation-religion in a world in which religion and nationality have tended to become divorced. But more important than this, religion has lost in the modern world the major position it has held throughout history. I do not plan to go into this vast subject, except to point out that the flourishing state of theology, the building of churches, and high attendance at religious services must not blind us to the fact that religion has suffered crushing blows and plays a completely different role in the world today from that which it played only a hundred years ago.

The great change is that hardly any significant number of people now interpret life in the terms proposed by the major religions. They no longer live for salvation, no matter how defined, but for life on this earth, in this world, interpreted in purely non-religious terms. There are Jewish thinkers fond of pointing to the fact that Judaism has always emphasized this life rather than the life beyond the grave, as if to suggest that this puts Judaism in a better position than Christianity in the modern world. But in so doing they deceive themselves. Judaism governed all the minutiae of life, not to enhance it in the way in which contemporary men wish to enhance it, but to fulfil the word of God. And insofar as it is inconceivable for modern man to live so as to fulfil the word of God (unless that word is bowdlerized—which many ministers of religion are happy to do), Judaism is as badly off as any other religion.

The cause of this change is another matter. It is not possible—even were I competent to do so—to prelude a study of a particular religious group in America with a full discussion of the state of religion in the modern world. I can only indicate my general point of view. It seems to me that science has had a devastating effect on religion. Many first-class minds have set themselves the problem of reconciling science and religion, and from a theoretical point of view some of these efforts may be successful. But neither these attempts to make science and religion lie down together nor even the friendly attitudes of distinguished scientists toward religion have prevented catastrophic declines in the influence of religion. For science, whatever the disclaimers of distinguished scientists, explains the world, which is what religion once did, and its explanation does not have any place for the notion of a non-earthly reality guiding man's course on earth. Under the impact of science, most people see no point to life beyond making it as pleasurable as possible.

But then, in addition to changing the explanation of the world, science also changes the world and thus makes the aim of a pleasurable life in this world, once a purely utopian idea for the masses of people, a real possibility. Scientific technology creates a world filled with material wealth, which offers to every individual the possibility of satisfying his material needs and to every nation the prospect of becoming great and strong. When the fulfilment of life is seen by individuals and nations as the acquisition of possessions, they have abandoned their traditional religions—regardless of what they do on Sunday or how many churches they build.

II

Beginnings of American Judaism
1654-1825

In 1654 a group of Jewish families, fleeing Portuguese persecution in Brazil, landed in New Amsterdam. There were Jews in the British colonies of North America even before that date—their names pop up here and there in court records and in other sources that have been carefully examined by students of early American Jewish history. But these few shadowy and fugitive figures on the North American continent before 1654 were not the founders of an American Jewish community.

To understand the events of 1654, we must go back more than 150 years before that date to 1492, which is known in Western history as the year in which Columbus discovered America and in Jewish history as the year in which the populous and wealthy Jewish community of Spain was expelled from that country. The Jews of Portugal were expelled in 1497. Many Jews then left Spain and Portugal to search in a still-closed medieval world for places where they might be permitted to settle, and communities of Spanish and Portuguese Jews were established in the countries around the Mediterranean. Many remained in Spain and Portugal, formally or actually converted to Christianity, though their neighbors suspected them of being Jews, and they suffered various restrictions. On occasion, some of them were seized by the Inquisition, tortured, and even burned. In 1654, the year with which American Jewish history begins, ten Jews were burned to death in Cuenca and twelve in Granada.

Some of these converted Jews, we know, sailed with Columbus, and others were among the first Spanish settlers in the New World. By 1570 the Inquisition was at work rooting out secret Jews on this continent, and the autos-da-fé began in the New World too. But nothing in history is so amazing as the persistence of the Spanish and Portuguese Jews; secret Jewish groups continued to exist in various places in the New World.

The largest and most prosperous of the communities that had been established by these refugee Spanish and Portuguese Jews was in Amsterdam. In the United Netherlands, Jews found the only country in western Europe in which they could dwell legally; for they had been banned from England and France as well as from Spain and Portugal. The history of the Jews of Amsterdam begins with that of Dutch independence in the 1590's, and the Jews of Amsterdam helped establish the world-wide Dutch commercial supremacy of the seventeenth century.

The Dutch could also count on the friendship and the assistance of the secret Jews living in the colonies of their enemies. In 1630 the Dutch conquered Recife and the area around it in eastern Brazil with the help of the secret Jews already living there. In addition to freedom, Recife offered many opportunities for Jews, and many emigrated there from Holland and elsewhere to form a large and flourishing community.

In 1654 the Portuguese recaptured Recife, and the Jews had to leave. Some of the refugees went north to the Dutch colonies in the Caribbean, where Jewish communities already existed. Many returned to Amsterdam. And some, as we have seen, landed in New Amsterdam to begin Jewish history on the soil of what was later to become the United States.

The Dutch, it seemed, were not hospitable everywhere, and Peter Stuyvesant, governor of the tiny trading post on the Hudson, wished to expel the small group of Jewish refugees. Their fate was in the hands of the West India Company in Amsterdam, proprietors of the colony. But this company had important Jewish shareholders, who urged the directors to allow the Jews to remain; these refugees had loyally supported the Dutch in Brazil, had fought with them against the Portuguese, and had lost all their possessions in the defeat. The company ruled that the Jews might stay and trade. The Jews of Amsterdam, who made it possible for the refugees to remain in New Amsterdam in 1655, excommunicated the Jewish freethinker Baruch Spinoza in 1656. We may better understand the beginnings of Jewish settlement in America by seeing it in the perspective of the Middle Ages than in the perspective of later American history.

New Amsterdam (in 1664 to become New York) was the first of a number of Jewish communities that, in time, were to dot the eastern seaboard. Not long after the refugees settled in New Amsterdam, Newport, Rhode Island, received its first Jews. This community, which, we know, acquired a cemetery in 1677, may have disappeared toward the end of the seventeenth century; but by the mid-eighteenth century there was again a flourishing Jewish group, which dedicated its beautiful synagogue, a masterpiece of colonial architecture, in 1763. Before the end of the eighteenth century there were added to the settlements in New York and Newport communities large enough to found synagogues in Charleston, Savannah, Philadelphia, and Richmond. By that time there were between two and three thousand Jews in the United States, and in

Charleston the largest Jewish community in the United States numbered about five hundred souls.

This was the situation after almost 150 years of Jewish history in what is now the United States. Obviously we deal with a very miniature history, so miniature that it has been possible to track down almost every Jew who set foot on these shores.

In the beginning, these Jewish immigrants were "Sephardim," the term used to refer to Jews from Spain and Portugal and their descendants in other colonies. They came by way of Brazil, the Caribbean islands, Holland, and England. Sometimes they arrived directly from the Iberian Peninsula. As late as 1767, 275 years after the decree of expulsion, Abraham Lopez and his wife and three sons arrived in Newport from Portugal; his brother, to whom he came, wrote to a Jew in New York to come and circumcise Lopez and his sons.

But not long after the first Jews began to come to the American colonies, these Sephardim were joined by "Ashkenazim," the term used for Jews from Germany and their descendants in other countries. In the seventeenth and eighteenth centuries, most Ashkenazic Jews lived in Poland; in Amsterdam and in London, the Sephardic and Ashkenazic communities were rigidly separate. Their religious ritual differed in some small details. More important in keeping the two communities apart were the feelings of the Sephardim that they formed an aristocracy among Jews, and their refusal to mingle with poorer and to their minds uncouth coreligionists. But in the American colonies the Jewish aristocracy meant as little as others, and the two elements mingled with less self-consciousness. All five congregations established before the nineteenth century—in New York, Newport, Philadelphia, Savannah, Charleston, and Richmond—followed the Sephardic rite. Probably in every one of them except Newport, Jews of

Ashkenazic origin predominated. The strong attachment to special rites that was to play so large a part in Jewish religious history in the nineteenth and twentieth centuries did not appear during the first 150 years. Presumably the Ashkenazic—like the Sephardic—immigrants of those years were the more cosmopolitan members of their groups in the Old World and were less attached to local peculiarities than those whom they had left behind in Europe.

In the seventeenth century, the European Jews could be described as a people of merchants and traders and some scholars. The Jews who came to the American colonies were drawn from the merchant and trader, not the scholarly, element. Some were storekeepers, artisans, doctors, even landowners; but the dominant tone of the Jewish communities was set by the merchants. They traded with the Indians, the Caribbean islands, Europe, and the other American colonies, and they furnished supplies for the armed forces. These were hazardous occupations at a time when the roads were uncertain and pirates, privateers, and enemy warships dominated the seaways, and when, in any case, it was all too easy for a ship to founder or a trusted associate to disappear. They led uneasy and unsettled lives. One can find Jews moving from one colony to another in search of opportunities; some languished in debtor's prison or appealed to the charity of more prosperous Jewish merchants. But one also finds wealthy Jewish merchants, who very likely had been poor a few years before and would be poor again. As merchants, these early Jews were more "visible" in colonial society than their tiny numbers would suggest, which is perhaps why it is possible for historians to find out so much about them. We find records of them in court proceedings, on lists of taxpayers, on petitions requesting some right or the lifting of some restriction, as we might expect in the age of mercantilism.

Beginnings of American Judaism

Politically, the situation of the Jews differed from colony to colony. In New Amsterdam they had to fight for the right to remain, to bear arms, to trade, to practice their religion publicly, and the situation was similar in other colonies. But for the most part the medieval restrictions that dominated the lives of Jews and the lives of others in Europe could not be successfully transferred to a new world. In 1740 an act of Parliament permitted the naturalization of Jews in the British colonies. By this time, the Jews enjoyed more freedom, legally and in fact, in the British colonies in America than anywhere else in the world.

No religious dignitaries and no learned men came to America; such men had no reason to emigrate. In 1773, we are told,[1] there were three rabbis in the New World: one in Jamaica, one in Surinam, one in Curaçao. There were none on the North American mainland. This reflected the fact that the Jews of the trading islands of the Caribbean were wealthier than the Jews of the northern trading towns on the coast. Indeed, when the Jewish community of New York decided in 1729 to build a synagogue, it wrote for assistance to the richer communities of the Caribbean; other congregations in later years did the same.

Theoretically, the absence of dignitaries is no bar to the establishment of a Jewish synagogue. Ten adult males are all that is required. The knowledge of the order of services and of Jewish ritual is not restricted to any group but is taught to all and learned by all. Still, religious leaders were essential. The "hazzan"—the prayer-chanter who leads the congregation in the service—tended more and more to play a role equivalent to that of minister in the Protestant groups, even though the office itself was of no great importance from the point of view of Jewish history or Jewish religion.

Together with the communities, the congregations in time became Americanized. The minutes of Congregation Shearith Israel of New York were recorded in Portuguese until 1736; the congregational accounts were kept in Portuguese until 1745; and the constitution and bylaws of 1749 were recorded in both English and Portuguese. This was the last recorded use of Portuguese in this congregation.

Though they were Americanized, in the sense that they used English exclusively, and though they lived like other colonial worthies—judging from their portraits, they looked like them and like them they fought, on both sides, in the Revolution—these early immigrants found no difficulty in remaining Jews. Here and there we read of isolated individuals who married non-Jews, who were perhaps converted, and whose children were brought up as non-Jews. The grandfather of John Howard Payne, who wrote "Home, Sweet Home," was such a Jew. From a modern perspective, we are surprised, not by the occasional cases of conversion and intermarriage, but rather by the great strength of these tiny communities and their ability to keep so large a proportion of the Jews closely attached to them.

We must try, however, to understand them from the perspective of the seventeenth, not the twentieth, century. From that perspective, we must see the synagogue not as an independent institution to take care of the "religious needs" of people but rather as the expression of a unified Jewish community. In the seventeenth and eighteenth centuries in Europe the Jews were organized into communities, recognized (and exploited) by the sovereign, but still they possessed certain rights of self-government. The community leaders managed the synagogue and appointed a communal rabbi, who was an official, not of the *synagogue*, but of the *community*. This rabbi determined questions of religious law, conducted Jewish schools, arranged for the baking of matzoth (unleavened bread) for Passover and the ritually correct slaughter of animals for meat. In

America, however, there could be no such legally recognized organization. In the colonies, the Jews had more or less the same position as other dissenting sects in that they were largely ignored by the governing authorities and free to determine their own character.

Nevertheless, from the Jewish point of view it seemed obvious that there should be such a community; and the synagogue, which in Europe was only one agency of the Jewish community, in this country became *the* community. As contrasted with the Jewish communities in Europe, the Jewish communities in America had no taxing power and could not call on the state authority to enforce their decisions. On special occasions and for brief periods the local synagogue may have had some semigovernmental powers. Thus Congregation Shearith Israel secured a local ordinance giving it the right to supervise the ritual slaughtering of animals according to Jewish law. But even without such powers, the synagogue acted like a true community and did have a certain disciplinary power over the Jews. Social pressure could play some role in replacing official power, though not much, for in these tiny communities most Jews had many non-Jewish friends. (As late as 1773, there were only thirty Jewish families in New York.) Then, the congregations had a monopoly of certain religious rites. In particular, they controlled the cemeteries, and almost all Jews wished to be buried in hallowed ground. But more important than social pressure and the control of the cemetery was the fact that the idea of the community was then so universal in Jewish life that most Jews simply could not imagine living apart from it. This ubiquity of the idea of community is reflected in the financial help on numerous occasions expected and actually obtained from the Jewish congregations by Jewish merchants struck by disaster, or by poor Jews wandering through the colonies. In short, the individual Jew could not yet conceive of himself as totally separated from the group. And so the heads of the Jewish community could in turn make certain demands on Jews. They could insist that their members obey the dietary laws, be married by the "minister" of the congregation, attend services, and so on; and they actually secured some measure of obedience. In the minutes of the New York congregation one sees a synagogue ruled with an iron hand, regulating behavior, distributing fines and rewards, exacting obedience—all without stirring a rebellion that, under American conditions, would have been impossible to suppress.

The pattern of their religious life proper we might call dignified Orthodoxy. Those who are familiar with the Orthodoxy of the East European Jews, and particularly the characteristic disorder of its religious services (at least to the outsider's eyes), will understand why a distinguishing adjective is necessary to describe the religious life of the first American synagogues. They adhered strictly to the Sephardic ritual, at first as a matter of course but later, one suspects, because the early synagogues became proud of their ancient traditions. Congregation Shearith Israel established what was in effect a living museum of Sephardic practice. Its present handsome synagogue on Central Park West in New York City still houses relics of the first synagogue built near the tip of Manhattan Island 225 years ago. Naphtali Taylor Phillips, who served as clerk of Shearith Israel, and who died in 1927, was preceded as clerk by his father, who was preceded as clerk by his father. And his grandfather's great-grandfather was a court physician in Portugal who escaped from Lisbon in 1733. For a small community consisting mostly of well-to-do merchants and without a vigorous intellectual life, dignified Orthodoxy was an appropriate and viable pattern; it has lasted to this day.

About the time when the first Jews were coming to America,

Beginnings of American Judaism

Jews, Sephardic and Ashkenazic, were settling in Cromwellian England and establishing their synagogues. These, too, were small communities of merchants, and they also established a pattern of dignified Orthodoxy that has been maintained in England until today. Since the past has in general more authority in England than in America, this pattern has become that of English Jewry in general. The dignified Orthodoxy of the ancient Sephardic synagogues in the United States, on the other hand, influences only a small part of contemporary American Jewry.

This pattern could be maintained here only while communities remained small and while newcomers were willing to submit voluntarily to the order established by previous settlers. For no governmental authority in America had any desire to legislate for the Jewish community. In 1802, as a matter of fact, Jews of Ashkenazic background decided to found a new synagogue in Philadelphia, where there already existed a Sephardic synagogue. In 1825 the Ashkenazim in Congregation Shearith Israel, chafing under the strong administration of the leaders of the synagogue, decided to withdraw and form their own synagogue, B'nai Jeshurun. New York then had only five hundred Jews, but the number was soon to increase rapidly. B'nai Jeshurun was formed principally by English Ashkenazim, but it was not to be long before other Ashkenazic groups—Dutch, German, French, and others—felt strong enough to form their own congregations.

Not many immigrants were required to transform a community of five hundred souls. After the end of the wars in Europe in 1815, the flow of immigration that had been so often cut off in the preceding forty years resumed, and many Jews were among the immigrants. The colonial Jewish community had doubled by 1826, and the pattern of Jewish life established generations before in the colonies was by then rapidly changing.

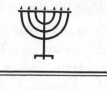

III

The German Immigration and the
Shaping of Reform
1825-94

The period between 1775 and 1815 was to be the longest given the American people to develop its character without the disturbing influence of great numbers of immigrants of varying backgrounds.

The American Jewish community, too, which had received relatively large numbers of immigrants during the 1750's and 1760's, was given time in which to blend its various elements. The original languages of the immigrants disappeared. This happened partly because the influence of any single language group in this mixed community was too slight to impose a single foreign tongue; partly because a large number of Jewish immigrants, whether Sephardic or Ashkenazic, had spent time in England and in English colonies in the Caribbean and so knew English. Thus the split in the synagogue of New York which produced the first New York Ashkenazic synagogue, B'nai Jeshurun, was initiated and led not by recent immigrants but by men fully as Americanized as those who remained in Shearith Israel.

But in a short while "Ashkenazic" was to become identified in America with recent German-speaking immigrants of low social status. Until 1836, Jewish immigration into America was almost entirely the immigration of individuals and isolated families, almost a random movement, in which each individual, for a variety of individual reasons, had made his own decision to emigrate. In 1836 there began the first *mass* migration to America. By "mass migration" I mean a movement of whole families and groups of families, from a single locality or country, owing to influences which affect an entire community, and the individual through the community.

The circumstances of the Jews in most of the German states in the early nineteenth century made them ripe for emigration. The Jews tended to be artisans and small traders and merchants scattered through the towns with no great concentrations in the cities. They suffered under a load of special taxes and restrictions, which not only were humiliating but affected their chances of business success and even of personal happiness. In Bavaria, for example, in order to control the number of Jews in each town, the number of marriages that might be contracted by Jews was limited by law!

In 1836 these conditions, combined with a slump in trade, finally led to an emigration movement among the Bavarian Jews. This was the beginning of a continual and steady movement of German Jews to the United States; though halted briefly by the American Civil War in the early 1860's, it did not cease until the last decades of the century. The American Jewish population was estimated at 15,000 in 1840, 50,000 in 1850, 150,000 in 1860, and 250,000 in 1880. By the last year, the American Jewish community was almost entirely a German community. For even those immigrants who did not come from Germany itself had emigrated from lands under German cultural influence (Austria, Bohemia, Hungary, and western Poland) and spoke German.

Socially, the new immigrants were on a lower level than the seventeenth- and eighteenth-century immigrants. The earlier arrivals we have called "merchants." The new German immigrants, who also belonged to that caste of traders that the Jews, Sephardic and Ashkenazic alike, had become by the seventeenth century, could only be called "merchant" by courtesy. Many of the earlier immigrants had arrived with important connections among merchant families in England, Holland, and the Caribbean. The new immigrants came without important business connections, were generally very poor, and were financially incapable of entering into wholesale trade. Many of them became peddlers, in the cities and through the countryside, and many left the seaboard cities to strike inland. They peddled in the South, beyond the Appalachians, in the Midwest, and in the Far West, where Jews were among the first settlers in many towns. Where they could, they established clothing and drygoods and general stores. They arrived when the country was expanding, and they followed its routes of expansion. Most of the Jewish communities of this country were established by these small groups of German Jewish peddlers.

In 1825 there were only about a half-dozen active congregations in the United States; by 1848 there were about fifty, largely German Ashkenazic. These congregations introduced into American Jewish life what was almost the first tremor of intellectual conflict and dissension it had ever known. The placid Orthodoxy of the old settlers was swamped by a variety of conflicting forms of Judaism struggling with each other for the domination of the American Jewish community. To understand the nature of this conflict, we must go back to the Germany the immigrants had left. It was there that the great struggle between Reform and tradition was begun.

I have already spoken of the self-governing European Jewish community that had developed in the Middle Ages and still existed in central and eastern Europe. Most of the internal law of this community had been, until the end of the eighteenth century, in large measure the law worked out by the rabbis of Palestine and Babylonia between the second and sixth centuries of the Christian Era, the law summed up in that enormous compilation, the Talmud, and interpreted by succeeding generations of rabbis. This law governed not only what we would consider the religious behavior of the Jew in every detail, such as what prayers should be said and when and in what manner, but also other aspects of life—what can be eaten and how, what kind of clothing may be worn, and in what way one is to prevent ritual impurity. Also, insofar as governments did not interfere, the Talmudic or Rabbinic law decided questions of marriage, divorce, adoption, inheritance. Many parts of this law had fallen into disuse by the end of the eighteenth century. Obviously, Jews no longer observed those parts dealing with the temple service and the priesthood or with agriculture. They could no longer enforce the criminal law, and the civil law was only partially observed (disputes over property could be be settled in the state courts).

The difficulty that the Talmudic law presented to Jews was its rigidity, which was a direct consequence of its presumed divine origin. Some of it was in fact to be found in the Bible, but by far the greater part had been elaborated by rabbis over the course of a thousand and more years—this part too, it was asserted, was immutable, enjoying the same authority as what had been revealed to Moses at Sinai. This viewpoint made it difficult to modify the law. The role of the rabbi, then, was not to legislate but to apply the law and interpret it. Even more complicating was the fact that Talmudic principles of long standing asserted that the customs of the Jews, a sacred people, also had legal authority and that customs which merely served to differentiate the Jews from other peoples could have legal authority for that reason alone. So that, for example, an attempt to change a custom like the wearing of the hat in the synagogue, which has neither Biblical nor Talmudic authority, could be and was denounced as impious.

Until the French Revolution, the Jews had almost everywhere considered themselves, and had been considered, a separate nation, governing themselves, to whatever extent the constituted state authority permitted, by the Talmudic law. The Jews offered a perplexing problem to an enlightened monarch who wished to strike off their medieval shackles and make them another religious denomination of his realm: Frenchmen or Germans or Austrians of the Jewish persuasion. Napoleon, for example, was at a loss to understand the status of the Jews. The French Revolution had emancipated the Jews in France and the rest of the Napoleonic Empire—Holland, Italy, and western Germany. But did they consider themselves *Frenchmen?* In 1806 Napoleon called a meeting of Jewish dignitaries from France and the German and Italian lands that had become part of his empire to answer a series of questions on this point, and some of these questions were most embarrassing: for example, did Jewish law, regardless of the civil status decreed for the Jews, forbid intermarriage with non-Jews? These Jewish notables wished to be French citizens and to be relieved of the load of special laws imposed on them by foreign rulers. But their own special laws—and they were *religious* laws—treated them as a separate nation and enjoined their strict separation from the non-Jews. The members of this assembly, however, not being strongly devoted to the Jewish law, were able to give Napoleon satisfactory answers. If his assembly of Jewish leaders had been from east of the Elbe, the story would have been quite different.

By 1815, particularly as a result of the French conquests, the Jews of central Europe had become in some measure "emancipated," from both the rules imposed by others and the rules of their own religion. They could now take up life as Frenchmen or Germans or Austrians of the Jewish persuasion. We are not to conceive of the German Jews, who are our main concern, as suddenly in the nineteenth century emerging from the medieval cave, blinking their eyes. There had already been a number of Jews, individuals connected with princely courts, great merchants and bankers, and scholars like Moses Mendelssohn (1729–86), who had, before and during the period of the French Revolution, become "modern men." They received secular as well as traditional educations, made friends among non-Jewish intellectuals, and, in brief, experimented in leading lives in the contemporary world while still remaining Jews. Indeed, some Jewish ladies even held salons for intellectuals in Berlin.

Under these circumstances, many Jews in the early nineteenth century in Germany were embarrassed by their ancient law and ambiguous status. In particular, they found their religious services distasteful for persons aspiring to the status of full members of the German nation. "Reform" Judaism began as a movement of Jews of high social status who wished to dignify Jewish religious services and make them decorous. They did not like the idea that the traditional Jewish service was (among the Ashkenazim) a rather cacophonous Hebrew outpouring by the congregation, dressed in hats and prayer shawls, and led by a cantor (prayer-leader) using a decidedly un-Western and un-Germanic mode of singing, or rather chanting. And then, too, there was nothing that might be understood as edification in this service, for there was no sermon; twice a year the rabbi (generally drawn from Poland, that great well of Talmudic learning) would deliver a barely intelligible discussion of some Talmudic problem.

Discontented with the traditional services, laymen, and some rabbis, began to experiment with new services in the second decade of the nineteenth century in various places in Germany. At Seesen in 1810, in Berlin in 1815, and, most important, at Hamburg in 1818, services were conducted in which a good part of the prayers were read in German, some were cut, an organ was used, and a preacher delivered sermons in German.

The early Reformers also attacked traditional Jewish education, which consisted almost solely of the learning of the Bible and the Talmud. Again, they were made uncomfortable by the fact that there was little that could be considered morally edifying in this type of schooling. They set up a number of modern schools, modeled on Protestant schools, and replaced the Bar Mitzvah, the rite by which a Jewish boy becomes subject to the commandments, with a confirmation, a ceremony in which boys and girls participated and which indicated that one had absorbed a certain minimum of moral and ethical education.

While many of these things were not prohibited in the "written" or "oral" law (that is, the Bible or the Talmud), all the changes were violently attacked by Orthodox rabbis. But German Orthodoxy was already weak. In the early nineteenth century many German Jews were converting to Christianity. The children of Moses Mendelssohn himself, who had argued that it was possible to be a Jew in every way while participating in the general, non-Jewish life, became Christians. Many argued that Reform might serve to check the wave of conversions.

The issues between the Reformers and the traditionalists in the beginning dealt largely with the public face of Judaism—its services and their nature and the possibility of adapting them to the Western norm for religious services. But inevitably the battle over the practical reforms, some of which did come into conflict with specific Talmudic prohibitions, spread to the realm of thought. Here, traditional Judaism was helpless. All the supposed sharpness and subtlety of the Jewish mind had for hundreds of years been devoted to the truly "Talmudic" elaboration of the law; its basis had never been questioned. As long as the world in general did not question the divine authority of the Bible, the Jews could put up a respectable intellectual defense against Christian attacks. But once the text of the Bible became subject to critical study, once the question was raised of whether the Bible really did incorporate God's commands, the foundations of Jewish thought, such as they were in the eighteenth century, crumbled.

As long as Reform consisted of a largely opportunistic desire to adapt to Western norms, and this seemed characteristic of the initial efforts at modernizing, it could be fought respectably by the traditionalists. But by the 1830's the first fumbling efforts at practical Reform had been succeeded by a very extensive critical attack on traditional Judaism. And once the traditional position could be attacked as wrong as well as inconvenient, as based on an illusion or a lie, the traditionalists were helpless. The young Jewish intellectuals of Germany at the time—the generation of Heinrich Heine and Karl Marx—were passionate followers of reason and the ideals of the French Enlightenment and were the sharpest possible opponents of traditional religion. Their personal convenience coincided with their perception of the truth, and they became either Reformers, radicals, or Christians (Heine became all three, at different times). If young Christian intellectuals turned against traditional religion in Germany during the second, third, and fourth decades of the nineteenth century, how much more might we expect young Jewish intellectuals to attack revealed religion? Jews were after all far more strongly attracted to the new trends in thought because it was the political and religious philosophy of the Enlightenment that had brought about their freedom from medieval restrictions.

For this reason, among others, all those tendencies of thought that in the early nineteenth century challenged Enlightenment thinking and suggested a new foundation for religion had very little influence among Jews. I speak of the romantic and conservative reaction against rationalism in the early nineteenth century, which took various forms: the scholarship that examined ancient documents, myths, folklore, and folk practices and found in them more than simple childish irrationality; the politics that saw virtue in the old and established; the culture that was prejudiced in favor of the past and the practices of the people. The Jews could not embrace such tendencies, generally tied up with reaction and anti-Semitism. The position of the Jews in modern society was just one of those symptoms of the breakdown of tradition which romantics opposed. The defenders of traditional Judaism, accepting neither the rationalism of the Enlightenment nor the reaction of Romanticism, were thus left without intellectual weapons of any force among Jewish intellectuals and had to battle the Jewish rationalism of the nineteenth century with the weapons of the Middle Ages.

The intellectual justification of Reform took two forms. First, some Jewish scholars, of whom the principal ones were Leopold Zunz (1794–1886) and Abraham Geiger (1810–74), decided to devote themselves to scholarly investigations into the history of the Jewish religion to see whether greater knowledge could justify various proposed reforms. This kind of scholarship had never existed among the Jews, nor, indeed, had there been much of it among the Christians. A movement called the "Wissenschaft des Judentums" was thus begun that produced many important works and showed that some of the reforms proposed resembled in some ways the practices of the past. Thus, Zunz, in his *Die Gottesdienst-lichen Vorträge der Juden* (1832), showed that preaching in the vernacular was no revolutionary innovation in Judaism.

However, scholarship alone could not possibly justify enough reforms to satisfy those who wished to westernize Judaism. The basic problem was the whole structure of Jewish law and its divine origins. Various Jewish thinkers tried to dispose of the embarrassing shackles of the complex code of Talmudic legislation. Some asserted that only the Bible really had divine authority, but that was no help, for even the Bible contained laws that were repugnant to a modern Westerner. The tendency developed among the German Reformers to emphasize the progressive nature of Jewish law, the fact that it had, indeed, developed and changed continually in response to different conditions. However, there was no question that the course of development they were proposing quite reversed the history of the law up to that time, for until then it had developed in the direction of ever greater complexity, and what the Reformers were proposing was a radical simplification. However, one could also find among the German Reformers the position that the law was simply outgrown and that Judaism should base itself on the prophetic and not the legal portions of the Bible. And since a number of prophets had indeed emphasized social justice and ethical behavior and had attacked priestly rites, they seemed well suited to serve as forerunners of Reform Judaism.

The German Jewish migration to this country had originally consisted of the more impoverished and less educated members of the German Jewish population, who were scarcely affected by the battle over reform in the upper strata of German Jewish society. In the 1840's and 1850's, however, many persons from the more prosperous and better educated parts of the German Jewish population began to come over to America. A number of rabbis who had already played some role in the fight over reform, or had at least been affected by it, also came. Their influence was great. They were in one sense the first rabbis to come to this country—that is to say, they had had regular rabbinic ordination, which none of the many ministers of Congregation Shearith Israel, for example, had ever had. Some of them had been educated in German universities and had earned German degrees. Their flocks were on the whole ignorant, both in Jewish matters and in secular knowledge. Their only opponents, at least to begin with, were the leaders of the old Sephardic and Ashkenazic synagogues, of whom the chief was Isaac Leeser (1806–68, hazzan of Congregation Mikveh Israel in Philadelphia, 1829–50, and editor of the *Occident* from 1843 until his death). As a result, men like Leo Merzbacher, who arrived in 1841, Max Lilienthal (1845), Isaac Mayer Wise (1846), David Einhorn (1855), Samuel Adler (1857), and others had a large and fertile field for their reforming labors. As Isaac Mayer Wise described the situation in 1848: "The majority of our congregations in this country have been established but a few years back; they are generally composed of the most negative elements of all the different parts of Europe and elsewhere; they have been founded and are now governed for the most part by men of no considerable knowledge of our religion. . . ."[1]

While such men would have the stubbornness and devotion to tradition of the ignorant, they could also be shown that what they were most attached to was superstition rather than a basic tenet of religion. Some, too, might be proud to become the instrument of a learned rabbi who spoke with the authority of the religious and secular education of the admired homeland. And those congregations that numbered a higher proportion of educated men would be affected by the spirit of the age, particularly as it showed itself in Germany, and their education would lead them to be Reformers, not more competent traditionalists.

So, here and there during the 1840's and 1850's, small groups of German Jews in the United States banded together in "Reform Vereine" ("Reform societies") which would in time become "temples," as the Reformers preferred to call their synagogues. To these temples came distinguished German rabbis, already in America or summoned directly from Germany. Har Sinai of Baltimore was the first congregation formed in this way (1842). Others were Emanuel of New York (1845) and Sinai of Chicago (1858). Sometimes an Orthodox congregation would find itself with an energetic rabbi who would stimulate a Reform-minded element either to introduce reforms or, if defeated, to secede and form a new congregation. This is what happened in Albany after the arrival of Isaac Mayer Wise in 1846. Around such issues as the installation of an organ, the use of mixed choirs (either of men and women or of Jews and Gentiles), the quantity of Hebrew in the service, the use of English or German translations of the Hebrew prayers, the family pew arrangement (as against the traditional separation of women in an upstairs balcony)—around these issues desperate battles were fought that at times came into the civil courts as one group or another challenged the legality of elections or appealed to the courts to uphold a congregational constitution. The details of this struggle can be found in many congregational histories.

Interestingly enough, the struggle for Reform was far more successful in America than in Germany, primarily because of the absence of anything like a community structure for Jewish life in this country. In Germany, the Reform element was faced with central communal bodies in each city that appointed the rabbis for the community synagogue. These bodies were recognized by the government, and the service of the synagogue, in many states, was regulated by the government. The existence of a community meant often that a complete victory was necessary before there could be any recognition of the laymen's desire for Reform. The Reformers could not simply secede from the synagogue: either because they would hesitate to destroy the unity of an ancient and established community or because the government, suspicious of any innovation, would refuse to recognize them and put difficulties in their way.

And then the conservative element could appeal to the government, to prevent even a majority Reform element from instituting any changes. In the United States, even the kind of informal community that had existed around each synagogue before 1825, and for a while after that date, gradually broke down until each synagogue, and every group that wished to form one, was a law completely to itself, a possibility always inherent in the extreme congregationalism of Judaism.

The case of New York reveals how, as new synagogues sprouted (there were seventeen by 1853–54), the community disintegrated more and more, and the functions of each synagogue, at one time almost identical with that of a community, became less important. As the number of synagogues increased, it became impossible jointly to administer the ritual slaughter of animals and the baking of matzoth, and these functions were gradually taken over by commercial butchers and bakers. For a while, education was the responsibility of the synagogues, for the public school system was not well established and in any case Jews feared the teaching of Christianity in schools conducted by Christians. But in 1853, when the city of New York took over the schools of the Public School Society following the state law of 1842 which forbade religious instruction in public schools, the ambitious schools of a number of New York synagogues collapsed. The synagogue schools of other cities fared no better, and Jewish religious education limped along with a few Sunday hours. Charity, originally in New York the responsibility of Congregation Shearith Israel, paralleled later by the other synagogues that sprang from it, became divorced from the synagogues and was conducted by independent organizations. Finally even the cemeteries, originally, as we have seen, an important arm of the quasi-communal authority of the synagogue, became separated from the synagogue.

German Immigration and Shaping of Reform

The development of Jewish communities with no over-all headship, centrally or locally, with many synagogues and many uncoordinated institutions dealing with the different aspects of Jewish life, made the task of the Reformers easier. No awesome responsibility was undertaken when one founded a new synagogue or split an old one, and both practices soon resulted in a very large number of synagogues showing a great variety of practices.

We have spoken of Reform Judaism as being a purely immigrant phenomenon, and indeed it was the synagogues of the German immigrants that brought Reform Judaism into American life. There was, however, one harbinger of Reform of purely native character. In 1824, in Charleston, South Carolina, then as important as any Jewish community in America, a group of members of the old Orthodox Sephardic synagogue (Congregation Beth Elohim, founded in 1750) proposed reforms. These were quite moderate: they requested that some Hebrew prayers be repeated in English, that the service be abridged, that there be an English discourse on the text of the Torah reading each week. Their requests were denied, and the dissatisfied group, aware of developments in Germany, created a Reformed Society of Israelites. Under no need to compromise, they soon developed in a radical direction. Their statement of principles published in 1831 reads in part: "They subscribe to nothing of rabbinical interpretation, or rabbinical doctrines. They are their own teachers, drawing their knowledge from the Bible, and following only the laws of Moses, and those only as far as they can be adapted to the institutions of the Society in which they live and enjoy the blessings of liberty."[2] Here was full-fledged Reform, on native soil, conducted by native Americans. (One of their leaders, Isaac Harby, was a leading dramatist and journalist, and one of his plays was acted before President Monroe in Charleston in 1819.) Although they took their lead from the example of the

Hamburg Temple, one of the first efforts at practical Reform in Germany, their accent was authentically American.

This society wound up its affairs in 1833, and the members returned to Congregation Beth Elohim. But by 1840, when the old Charleston synagogue burned and the question of rebuilding it arose, the Reformers had gained the upper hand and voted for an organ. Now the traditional element seceded, and even went so far as to take its case to the courts. This new and successful attempt at Reform was led by a Polish-born, German-educated rabbi of Congregation Beth Elohim and soon became part of the general wave of Reform that began to make itself felt throughout the country under the influence of other immigrant German rabbis.

Of these reforming rabbis, Isaac Mayer Wise (1819–1900) was undoubtedly the most important, and the story of American Reform can best be told by way of his career. Wise arrived in this country from Bohemia in 1846 with a fairly good Talmudic education (though some dispute this), a smattering of secular education, and the strong intention of continuing the work of Reform, in which he felt checked in Europe. He had become disgusted with the petty annoyances put in his way by the rabbinic authorities of Bohemia, who were backed by state authority. He acquired a congregation in Albany, where he soon came into conflict with the conservative element.

From the beginning he had great plans. He wished to unify American Jewry, and as early as 1849 (following an earlier effort of Leeser in 1841) he joined with Leeser in issuing a call for a national federation of the rapidly increasing number of synagogues. Like most such efforts since, it came to nothing. He also wished to establish a modernized Hebrew prayer book, to be used uniformly in all the American synagogues, a "Minhag America" ("American ritual"), to replace the Sephardic and Ashkenazic rituals, and as early as 1847, in a meeting of rabbis in New York, he had himself assigned to this task. He also wished to establish an American institution for the training of rabbis. In pursuit of this aim, he left Albany, which was split by his efforts at Reform, in 1854 to become the rabbi of a congregation in Cincinnati that offered to make itself his instrument.

To understand Wise, we must see him above all as an Americanizer. He had a passion for America as the land of freedom. It permitted him to do whatever he wished without restriction. On his arrival in this country, he threw himself into the job of learning English with ferocious energy. "In the early 1850's," writes a student of this period, "there were only five rabbis in the United States who had a full command of English,"[3] and Wise was one of them. Most of his fellow Reformers still preached and wrote in German. On his arrival in Cincinnati, he immediately established an influential weekly, in English, the *American Israelite*, to serve as his organ and to oppose Leeser's *Occident*. At its side he established a German weekly, for, whatever his feelings about the need to Americanize Jewry, German was still the language of the great majority of American Jews. He wrote many books, including novels, as well as a good part of his two newspapers.

In true American fashion, Wise cared little for ideas. And to mollify Leeser and introduce his hoped-for unity into American Israel, he was perfectly willing to accept the Talmud as "the only legally binding interpretation of the Bible" at a rabbinical conference in Cleveland in 1855. It is hardly possible he really believed this, even at that time.

Gradually Wise's plans came to fruition. In 1857, he published the first edition of his *Minhag America*, to the outrage of Leeser and the conservative elements. With the passing years, this prayer book, and others even more radical, gradually began to be used by more and more American synagogues, as local Reform elements in each of them took the ascendancy. In 1873, after a series of rabbinical conferences, Wise founded the Union of American Hebrew Congregations to serve as the organization of the modernized congregations. More and more synagogues adhered to this national union, even many that were later to be prominent in the opposition to Reform. Finally, in 1875, he opened Hebrew Union College in Cincinnati, the first successful attempt to found a school of higher Jewish education in America. Leeser and other conservative rabbis had founded Maimonides College in Philadelphia for this purpose in 1867, but this institution closed in 1873.

From a list of about two hundred major congregations in existence in 1881, drawn up by Allen Tarshish,[4] it can be estimated that perhaps a dozen were still Orthodox by that year. Considerably more had adopted only a few major reforms, and there were scores of small congregations, not in this list, that were Orthodox. In 1872, there were already twenty-nine eastern European Orthodox synagogues in New York, most of them, of course, tiny. About half the major congregations that resisted Reform were the old Sephardic and Ashkenazic congregations that had been in existence before the beginning of heavy German immigration in the 1830's. With their great social prestige and their devoted members, they could afford to remain unaffected by the demands for modernization and westernization that were so effective among the immigrant Germans. Around 1880, even these old and conservative congregations were members of the Union of American Hebrew Congregations.

In 1879 the Union absorbed an earlier organization, the Board of Delegates of American Israelites. This organization had been formed on the model of the central organization of English Jews, in reaction to the Mortara case of 1858, in which a Jewish boy in Italy had been kidnapped and baptized. The Board of Delegates was the prototype of the present-day Jewish defense organization whose major purpose is to protect Jewish rights. After this merger, the Union was closer to being the dominant organization in American Jewish life than any other organization has ever been. In the early 1880's, after some forty years of conflict, it would have appeared to a superficial observer that the homogeneous and unified Jewish community of the 1830's had been restored, and on a much larger scale. This achievement could be credited to the energy and organizational skill of Isaac Mayer Wise.

Wise represents the first stage of Reform, in which its concern is purely practical and primarily with the modernization of the service, as we can see by his indifference to any formulated theoretical position. But, as we saw in the case of Germany, inevitably the problem of a theoretical justification for Reform arises, and this was not a task for the practical Americanizer.

Other Reformers were less American and less pragmatic. The leader of the more intellectual and, it turned out, more radical group of American Reformers, from the time of his arrival in the United States in 1855 until his death in 1879, was David Einhorn (born 1809). Einhorn, as one might expect of a rabbi interested in establishing a sound theoretical foundation for Reform, was passionately attached to the German language. Not only did he refuse to preach in English but he regarded the language with suspicion. As he wrote in his journal *Sinai* (which he published from 1856 to 1862): "It takes little familiarity with the condition of American Jewish religious life to recognize that the English element under present circumstances is a brake to Reform strivings. German research and science are the hearth of the Jewish Reform idea, and German Jewry has the mission to bring life and recognition to this thought on American soil."[5]

Einhorn was a German liberal and strongly opposed to slavery.

Indeed, he was forced to flee Baltimore at the beginning of the Civil War. It is equally expressive of the pragmatic temperament of Isaac Mayer Wise that, though a lover of American freedom, he was cautious about the slavery question.

It was largely under Einhorn's influence that the main points in the theoretical position for American Reform Judaism were to be worked out. The two major problems were the status of the divine law, which was settled by the argument that Judaism was progressive, and the status of the Jews in Western society. The latter was indeed a thorny question. Were they still a *people*, required to consider themselves strangers in all the countries in which they were settled and expecting to return to Palestine? Or were they a *religion* like all other religions, with a set of beliefs, and with no organic connection to a people?

In America, this was not yet a practical issue (perhaps it would never be) and Isaac Mayer Wise had never bothered about it. In Germany, it was a very vital issue, or so it was felt to be by the Reformers from the beginning, for the withholding of full rights of citizenship from the Jews, they thought, was based on the fact that the Jews were not Germans but a people who considered themselves in exile. When the Reformers vigorously denied this, certain things followed. They felt it necessary to delete all those prayers in the Jewish prayer book in which one prays to God to restore his people to the Land of Israel. This they did. They also felt it necessary to consider just what the Jews were doing in the Diaspora, for they could not accept the traditional view that the Jews had been exiled from Palestine for their sins. The Reform position, basing itself on some passages in Isaiah, was that the Jews had been sent out into the world by divine providence, not as a punishment, but to teach the true faith to the unenlightened. This idea of the "mission" of the Jews became very important in Reform Jewish thinking. To Reform Jews it explained why the Jews still persisted as a separate people; they had their mission to fulfil.

It was along these and similar lines that Einhorn and other radical Reformers in America thought. Einhorn felt that effective organization and the reform of the public service were far from sufficient. In Germany itself, Reform had been brought to a standstill by the 1850's because of the inherent conservatism of German Jewry, the German state, and German society and because of the obstacles presented by the communal organization of German Jewry. In America, the German Reformers continued their theoretical work. In 1869, Einhorn and a number of other eastern Reform rabbis of radical views met in Philadelphia under the chairmanship of Rabbi Samuel Hirsch (1815–89), who had arrived in America only three years before and held an important position among the radical thinkers in the Reform group. This conference declared, among other things, that "the messianic aim of Israel is not the restoration of the old Jewish state . . . but the union of all the children of God"; further, that they looked upon the destruction of the Jewish state "not as a punishment for the sinfulness of Israel but as a result of the divine purpose . . . [of dispersing] the Jews to all parts of the world for the realization of their high priestly mission, to lead the nations to the true knowledge and worship of God."[6] The statement was, of course, issued in German.

The finished platform of Reform Judaism in America was adopted sixteen years later in Pittsburgh at a conference called by Kaufmann Kohler (1843–1926), the son-in-law of the then deceased Einhorn. This platform was to be adopted a few years later by the Reform rabbinate. With admirable terseness and directness it summed up the final position arrived at by the Reform movement. It was a more radical statement than any that had ever been adopted in Germany and the logical culmination of the movement which had begun there.

In sum, the statement asserted that Judaism was a "progressive religion, ever striving to be in accord with the postulates of reason" and capable of changing its form in accordance with the advance of knowledge. The chief changes demanded by the modern age were the rejection of all Mosaic laws which "are not adapted to the views and habits of modern civilization" and the rejection of any national aim or national character for Judaism. "We consider ourselves no longer a nation, but a religious community, and therefore expect neither a return to Palestine, nor sacrificial worship under the sons of Aaron, nor the restoration of any of the laws concerning the Jewish state." (See the complete platform in the Appendix.)

Reform was now equipped with an organization of congregations, a seminary, and a platform. In 1889 Wise capped the structure by forming the Central Conference of American Rabbis, an organization of the Reform rabbis; and in 1894 the union of Wise's practicality and Einhorn's theoretical radicalism was symbolized by the publication of the *Union Prayer Book* by this body of rabbis. This was a far more radical prayer book in its drastic editing of the prayers and its almost complete elimination of Hebrew than Wise's had been. Nevertheless, he accepted it, and all American Reform followed him.

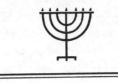

IV

Reformers and Conservatives
1880-1900

In the course of the forty-year struggle between the adherents of Reform and the adherents of Orthodoxy among the German Jews in America, the German Jewish community rapidly learned English and rose in the social scale. Arriving poor and often unlearned, the German Jews found conditions in a growing America economically favorable. Every burgeoning midwestern city offered opportunities for a few Jews to make fortunes in merchandising and for larger numbers to make a decent middle-class living as shopkeepers. In the South, small communities of Jewish merchants were established, and, in the Far West, individual Jews settled as merchants, again with success. In the East, a hierarchy of German Jewish society grew up, headed by a few wealthy families in banking and merchandising, and comprising a large and prosperous middle class which included many lawyers, doctors, and persons in public and intellectual occupations. By the end of the nineteenth century Jewish congressmen, judges, and college professors were not uncommon.

After forty years of settlement in this country, the average economic and social level of the whole German Jewish group was extraordinarily high. In 1880 the Jewish community numbered about 250,000. Unlike the community we know today, it was not heavily concentrated in the largest cities and in the Northeast. In the West, where they were spread as merchants through every town, the Jews formed 1½ per cent of the population, whereas in the Northeast only about one-half of 1 per cent of the population were Jews. Before the Civil War, there was also very likely a higher proportion of Jews among the white population of the South than in the Northeast. Throughout the country Jews appeared in every small town that served as a trading center for an agricultural population. If an area declined, or another area showed more promise, the Jews would move on; and so, toward the end of the century, the large cities showed a growing concentration of German Jews, as of the population in general.

A demographic survey of a large part of the long-settled German Jewish population was conducted by the federal government in 1890. Almost half the men were in business. One-fifth were accountants, bookkeepers, clerks, collectors, agents. One-tenth were salesmen, one-twentieth in the professions. One out of eight were skilled workers. Perhaps one-half of 1 per cent were laborers, and one out of a hundred, peddlers. Their high economic status was indicated by the fact that 40 per cent had one servant, 20 per cent had two, 10 per cent had three or more.

A Jewish community of a quarter-million people could support a vast number of organizations. In addition to 270 congregations in 1880, there were Jewish philanthropic organizations, fraternal orders, Jewish hospitals, and charitable bodies of all kinds. The most important national organization was the Union of American Hebrew Congregations.

This wide variety of institutional activity within the Jewish community did not, at least on the highest levels of Jewish society, mean that all Jewish social life was conducted within the Jewish community. All through this period, Jews were closely identified with Germans, and there was a good deal of social intermingling with non-Jewish Germans. But Isaac Leeser did not like the extravagant toast to the "German Fatherland"[1] at a banquet of the German Hebrew Benevolent Society of New York in 1853. The Germans, he pointed out, had still not granted equal civil rights to the Jews.

By the 1880's, many factors were operating to reduce contacts with the other German immigrants. The memory of the common experience of the revolution of 1848, which had bound together many Germans and Jews, had faded. The German immigrants tended to be farmers and artisans, while the Jewish immigrants were merchants and storekeepers. As the Jewish communities grew larger and formed their own organizations, diminishing numbers of Jews participated in the activities of the German organizations.

Also, the evidence suggests that, while the American upper class showed an easy acceptance of upper-class Jews through most of the nineteenth century, the 1880's began a period of increasing social exclusion. When the banker Joseph Seligman was refused admittance to the Grand Union Hotel in Saratoga in 1877, there was a wide outburst of indignation, and editorials were published in many newspapers attacking the hotel. But Richard Gottheil, in his biography of his father, Gustav Gottheil, rabbi of Temple Emanuel in New York, asserts that in the 1880's "private schools began to be closed to Jewish children. . . . Advertisements of summer hotels, refusing admittance to Jewish guests, commenced to appear in the newspapers."[2] And later: "In 1893, the Union League Club of New York had refused to admit Jews to membership."

Both parts of the picture—the increasing prosperity of the German Jews and their increasing sense of exclusion—are important in

American Judaism

understanding the great success of Reform Judaism among them. We must accept, at least in some degree, the characterization of nineteenth-century Reform as the religion of economically comfortable Jews who wanted to be accepted by the non-Jewish world. All the changes in ritual introduced by Reform brought Judaism closer to American middle-class Protestantism; but, again, this was not the only reason for the introduction of these changes.

The effect of these changes was to make the social atmosphere of the synagogue that of a Protestant church of the upper and upper-middle classes. Let us review some of the changes: The service was no longer read and sung by the congregation but read by the minister. Almost all of it was now in English. The congregation participated only in responsive readings and a hymn or two. Hats and prayer shawls were removed. An organ and a choir were introduced, and the choir usually included men and women instead of men and boys as in Orthodox practice. The balcony on which women sat, out of sight of the men, was removed, and men and women sat together. Some congregations even adopted a Sunday service. The main feature of the service became the sermon, in English. Judah L. Magnes (1877–1948), addressing Temple Emanuel in New York in 1910, said, "A prominent Christian lawyer of another city has told how he entered this building at the beginning of a service on Sunday morning and did not discover that he was in a synagogue until a chance remark of the preacher betrayed it."[3]

Outside the synagogue, too, the changes in the Jewish religion were all in the direction of stripping off every vestige of difference. Reform Jewish religious education consisted only of Sunday school. Almost all the distinctive Jewish rites were abandoned: At weddings no canopy was raised, no glass was broken. Special observances characterizing the various holidays were forgotten, and the cycle of religious festivals no longer created climaxes in the religious year.

A major reason for the rise of American, as of German, Reform was obviously the desire of prosperous laymen to acquire a religious service more in keeping with their social status. But other changes are not so easily explained. Consider the revision of the prayers in the *Union Prayer Book*. Here all references to the restoration of the temple service were removed, all references to the dispersion as exile or punishment, all prayers to God to rebuild Jerusalem and bring the Jewish people back to the Land of Israel. Now, during those years in which Reform triumphed, no one in America would have charged the Jews with being a nation apart, a peculiar people, if they had maintained these distinctive parts of the service; for in the America of the late nineteenth century the Jews were only one of many nations apart, one of many peculiar peoples. As we have pointed out, it was in Germany, where the fight for equal rights for Jews went on throughout the first half of the nineteenth century, that these references assumed importance. Why, then, did a change demanded by conditions in Germany become a reality in America?

It was primarily in order to bring the prayer book into conformity with the demands of a rationalistic philosophy that the rabbis deleted references that probably in America would have left both Jewish laymen and the non-Jewish world undisturbed. One cannot underestimate the sheer force of the rationalist and progressive position adopted by the rabbis, a position all of whose implications they worked out and tried to realize. And we must consider some consequences of this position, which, it turned out, contradicted the original intention of Reform, that is, to make Judaism a dignified, middle-class religion.

Reform had found in the prophets what it believed to be a more authentic tradition for Judaism. It was particularly attracted to two prophetic ideas: the idea that Judaism had a special mission in the world, which helped explain why the dispersion was not punishment; and the idea that social justice, which was first proclaimed as an ideal (at least with some vigor) by the Hebrew prophets, should particularly engage Jewish energies.

But consider the implications of these ideas, which became two of the cornerstones of American Reform Judaism: The first required that the Jews begin to carry out their mission to spread the knowledge of the true God. If they had been sent into the world with a religious mission, they should now become missionaries and begin to proselytize. This seemed the only alternative to considering the exile purely a misfortune, a traditional idea the Reformers had rejected. If the mission had been or was being accomplished by the monotheism of Christianity, what then was the *contemporary* function of Judaism? The second idea, that of social justice, demanded that the Jews, who in America were well-to-do middle-class merchants, should be in the forefront of the fight for social justice. And indeed, one of the points of the Pittsburgh Platform required them to do just that. The rabbis, or some of them, might accept the challenge, but what of the laity?

While the middle-class mass of Jews, who simply wanted a dignified service, resisted any such wild applications of the first principles of Reform, many rabbis did not, and they accepted the consequences of these positions. Proselytism was the least popular of the logical consequences of the Reform position. It has been proposed now and then, but as yet no Jewish missionary to the Gentiles has appeared in America. Some rabbis escaped this dilemma, and Judaism, by arguing that the mission had been to a large degree accomplished, for many non-Jews now accepted the true faith, namely, a humanistic ethical religion. There was consequently no reason to maintain Judaism; rather, the Jews should merge with all those trying to fulfil the mission. Thus, some Reform rabbis were forced by the logic of the Reform Jewish position to abandon Reform Judaism and become apostles of a religion of progress in which the distinction between religions and peoples was of no account. Felix Adler (1851–1933), son of Rabbi Samuel Adler (1809–91) of Temple Emanuel in New York, had been sent to Germany by Temple Emanuel to receive both a rabbinic and a secular education, with the idea that he would succeed his father as rabbi. He found, on his return to the United States in 1873, that he could not accept a distinctive Jewish religion as valid in the contemporary world; as a result, he founded the Ethical Culture Society in 1876. Though many non-Jews joined him in the work of the Ethical Culture Society, this movement was, in its origins and social composition, the direct outgrowth of Reform Judaism. It was one of the possible developments of Reform, and not the most unreasonable one.

At Temple Israel in Boston, one of the most important Reform synagogues in the country, two successive rabbis found they could no longer continue as ministers of the distinctive religion of a single people. If what Judaism had to say was only what any rational man inspired by a desire for justice and progress could accept, then why Judaism? So in 1893, Solomon Schindler, who was born in Germany in 1842 and, as rabbi of Temple Israel since 1874, had become a leader among Boston's non-Jewish reformers, left the pulpit to become a propagandist for the national socialism of Edward Bellamy. His successor, Charles Fleischer, born in Germany in 1871 and educated in the United States, was equally prominent among Boston's reformers, lay and clerical; in 1911, he also found even the Reform synagogue too confining and left to establish a community church in Boston.

Adler, Schindler, and Fleischer were exceptional cases, but they were in no sense cranks—they represented a significant tendency in Reform Judaism. Other rabbis could accept the idea that the religious mission of the Jew meant the service of truth, morality, and social justice without feeling in any way that this required them to give up their roles as Jewish ministers. On the other hand, rabbis like Stephen S. Wise, Judah L. Magnes, and Emil G. Hirsch who embraced social justice wholeheartedly might come into conflict, and often did, with the well-to-do among their congregants.

The ideological position that Reform forged, reflecting the rationalism and optimism of the second half of the nineteenth century, led the Reform rabbis, when they acted on the basis of theoretical considerations, into conflict with their congregations. Sometimes their ideology actually led them right out of Judaism; but, above all, it led to the serious weakening of Judaism as a religion.

I use the word "weakening," not from the point of view of any specific conception of Judaism, but only from the point of view that any religion is weakened if it does not have, in the simplest terms, the loyalty and close involvement of its members. The thoroughgoing rationalism of the Reform leaders put them in opposition to the complex structure of Jewish ritual practice which had maintained Jews as a people apart. The Reformers attacked and eliminated every ceremony, every ritual, every prayer that did not immediately and in a rather simple-minded way conform to their view of the truth (as defined by nineteenth-century scholarship) and so serve for spiritual and ethical uplift. The age-old practices of Judaism were consequently denounced as superstition, and any prayer that could not be believed literally was branded a lie no self-respecting man should be asked to repeat.

Thus, when a group of Jews intending to establish a Reform synagogue in Chicago wrote to Samuel Adler for advice, he answered: "I would state that the first and most important step for such a congregation to take is to free its service of shocking lies, to remove from it the mention of things and wishes which we would not utter if it had to be done in an intelligible manner. Such are, the lamentations about oppression and persecution, the petition for the restoration of the sacrificial cult, for the return of Israel to Palestine, the hope for a personal Messiah, and the resurrection of the body. In the second place, to eliminate fustian and exaggeration; and in the third place, to make the service clear, intelligible, instructive, and inspiring."[4]

His son, Felix Adler, was later to write: "Was I to act a lie in order to teach the truth? There was especially one passage in the Sabbath Service which brought me to the point of resolution: I mean the words spoken by the officiating minister as he holds up the Pentateuch scroll, 'And this is the law which Moses set before the people of Israel.' I had lately returned from abroad, where I had had a fairly thorough course in Biblical exegesis, and had become convinced that the Mosaic religion is, so to speak, a religious mosaic, and that there is hardly a single stone in it which can with certainty be traced to the authorship of Moses. Was I to repeat these words? It was impossible. It was certain that they would stick in my throat. On these grounds, the separation was decided on by me."[5]

As Beryl H. Levy, from whose excellent study of Reform Judaism these quotations are taken, says: "Of course, a less directly rational approach to liturgy would have allowed for congenial reinterpretation, appreciation of symbolic values and latitude for mythological and metaphorical expression. But the spirit bred by Reform, in its nobler expression, was nothing if not morally earnest, and attention to the lyric aptness, historical reverberations, or imaginative stimulation of a ritual form was not to be expected."[6]
And so, in the *Union Prayer Book*, two-thousand-year-old prayers

were ruthlessly chopped up and put together again, and new parts in harmony with the spirit of the age composed, generally by men whose English was not native.

It is hard for us to understand the simple-minded rationalism of the nineteenth century. Our era finds it easy to discover many meanings in poetry, myth, and folklore, and at least one acceptable meaning in any statement, no matter how paradoxical and meaningless it may appear on the surface. Yet the Reformers were not different in their way of thought from the ordinary Western intellectual of the nineteenth century. They were as much the product of their times as the primitive rites of Judaism had been the product of an earlier age. The idea that a form can have many contents was totally foreign not only to them but to every nineteenth-century man.

Reading the histories of local congregations, one is struck by the fact that at the end of the last century the individual congregations reached their lowest ebbs just when Reform Judaism, from the point of view of the development of its institutional structure and its ideas, had reached its finished form. Certainly there were many reasons for this. The first generation of German Jews, who combined acceptance of Reform with piety, was dying out; the children were rejecting perhaps not only their immigrant fathers but their immigrant fathers' religion. Religion in general in America seems to have reached a low point, and rationalism, socialism, and even atheism were strong throughout the country. Nevertheless, part of the reason for the lack of vitality among Reform congregations must be found in the character of Reform Judaism itself as it existed in its completed form at the turn of the century. Presented with the distilled essence of Judaism, the ordinary member of a Reform synagogue found not much of the old religion left.

Joshua Trachtenberg, in his excellent history of the congregation of Easton, Pennsylvania, thoughtfully considers the decline of this small German Jewish synagogue, which in 1896 had adopted the *Union Prayer Book* and abolished the use of German in the service. "The trouble lay not in Reform, but in Dutchtown [the German Jewish community] itself. Reform was a positive movement, with a distinct philosophy and theology. . . . There were Reformers who enhanced their appreciation of and devotion to Judaism by an intelligent and informed appraisal of its practices and values. But these were not to be found among the Dutchtowners. Because their conception of Reform was superficial and negative they were unable to retain the creative potential in the kernel whose shell they were stripping off. Where they had formerly, through their Jewish routine of life, espoused a Jewish conception of life, however unconsciously, when they rid themselves of that routine, with no philosophy other than expediency, they were left with no conception of life at all. Their ritual became for them dull and mechanical, their faith a colorless, lifeless recital of ideas and ideals that had never, in any event, meant too much for them. . . . Deficient as may have been their fathers' comprehension and appreciation of the essentials of their faith, it at least bound them to an ageless tradition that encompassed their lives with the illusion of comprehension."[7]

Around the turn of the century, it would not have been far-fetched for a historian of ideas to predict a merger between Reform Judaism and liberal Christianity. Reform rabbis annually met with Unitarian and Congregational ministers and liberal laymen in a Liberal Congress of Religion. The rabbis attending these conferences had far more in common with their liberal Protestant colleagues than they had with traditional Judaism. However, it could also be seen that the members of the dignified Reform congregations, in which the ministers spoke of a universal religion and social justice, were still made up largely of Jews who had no intention of being anything else and who were relatively unmoved by ideas and intellectual consistency. True, many of them intermarried with non-Jews and their children were not Jews. But the solid majority, while they claimed to be members of a religion, not a "people," reacted to pogroms and persecution abroad with somewhat more feeling than would have been justified by concern for coreligionists alone.

Even in the formulated positions of Reform Judaism there were interesting anomalies indicating that Reform rabbis were still held back by some kind of primal attachment to the Jewish people. Consider, for example, their attitude toward intermarriage with non-Jews. On what rational grounds could they oppose such intermarriage? For a religion that looked forward to the unity of mankind on the basis of prophetic justice, there would seem to be no possible objection to Jews marrying non-Jews, many of whom already accepted this outlook. Yet it was a rare Reform rabbi who took this position. Even radical Reformers like Einhorn opposed intermarriage. The Central Conference of American Rabbis also opposed intermarriage, declaring in 1909 that it was "contrary to the tradition of the Jewish religion and should therefore be discouraged by the American rabbinate."[8] Kaufmann Kohler, president of Hebrew Union College, who tried to present a complete theology for Reform, argued that "because of this universalistic Messianic hope . . . it is still imperative . . . that the Jewish people . . . continue its separateness . . . and . . . avoid intermarrying with members of other sects."[9]

An even more interesting anomaly is found in the Reform attitude toward circumcision. If one is interested in modernizing the Jewish religion, in bringing it into conformity with enlightened and progressive views, in abandoning any rite that does not serve to ennoble and uplift, the logical place to begin, one would think, is with circumcision. The requirement that male converts to Judaism be circumcised was indeed abandoned in one of the early meetings of the Central Conference of American Rabbis, but circumcision for the born Jew remained a part of Reform practice. So innocent and even edifying a ceremony as the Bar Mitzvah—whereby a male of thirteen is formally admitted as a full member of the community —was violently attacked by Kaufmann Kohler, and strong efforts were made to eliminate it from Reform practice. Yet circumcision remained.

The conclusion to all this must be that underneath the rational ideology of the leaders of Reform Judaism there still remained a simple unreflecting attachment to the Jewish people, a subconscious insistence that the Jews be maintained as a people. It was only this feeling that could have led to the retention of circumcision and to weak rationalizations of the traditional ban on intermarriage, which had indeed been so effective in maintaining the separateness of the Jewish people for eighteen hundred years. Still Jews, Reform laymen reacted with anger and compassion to the Russian pogrom at Kishinev in 1903 and organized the American Jewish Committee to protect Jewish rights throughout the world. And it was this loyalty to the Jewish people, which they had formally declared no longer existed, that led them to accept responsibility for the masses of East European Jews who began to come into the country around 1880.

The fact that Reform Jews still considered themselves implicitly members of the Jewish people should not lead us, however, to underestimate the gravity of the break that Reform, or more precisely nineteenth-century rationalism, had introduced into Judaism. The historical basis of Jewish unity is the law, and authority in the Jewish religion resides not in individuals but in the law as interpreted by the whole body of men whose education permits them to understand and interpret it. In the nineteenth century, and for the first time in Jewish history, qualified interpreters of the law rejected the traditional principles of interpretation and asserted that they could take upon themselves the right and the responsibility to create a new law. Such a claim, made any time in Jewish history up to the nineteenth century, had always meant exclusion from the body of the Jewish people.

The matter was not only theoretical. The Reform Jews, in a few decades or, at most, generations, had rapidly moved so far from the several-thousand-year-old norms of Jewish life that they were incapable of understanding the violence of the opposition from those who were still conservative or Orthodox. One example will indicate how far the Reform Jews had moved from the understanding of traditional practice. In 1883, the first class of Hebrew Union College in Cincinnati was graduated. At that time almost every synagogue of importance in the country was a member of the Union of American Hebrew Congregations, and rabbis who were later to lead a conservative resistance to Reform still thought of Hebrew Union College as an institution that might serve all American Jewry. We will let one of those who was graduated (David Philipson) tell what happened on this occasion:

"The convention of the Union of American Hebrew Congregations, whereof this rabbinical ordination was the peak, closed with a great dinner at a famed hilltop resort, the Highland House. Knowing that there would be delegates from various parts of the country who laid stress upon the observance of the dietary laws, the Cincinnati committee engaged a Jewish caterer to set the dinner. The great banqueting hall was brilliantly lighted, the hundreds of guests were seated at the beautifully arranged tables, the invocation had been spoken by one of the visiting rabbis, when the waiters served the first course. Terrific excitement ensued when two rabbis rose from their seats and rushed from the room. Shrimp [one of the forbidden foods, *terefa*] had been placed before them as the opening course of the elaborate menu. . . . The Highland House dinner came to be known as the '*terefa* banquet.' The Orthodox Eastern press rang the changes on the *terefa* banquet week in and week out. The incident furnished the opening to the movement that culminated in the establishment of a rabbinical seminary of a conservative bent."[10]

One suspects that the reason this incident has not been referred to by historians of the origins of the movement now called Conservatism is that it is embarrassing to trace such great consequences to the serving of shrimp, and in any case the adoption of the Pittsburgh statement by the Reform group in 1885 was at least as important in spurring the Conservatives to action. Yet the incident reminds us once again of the dominant role of traditional practice in Judaism. Certainly the Pittsburgh Platform led to a sharp reaction; but one can be sure that the serving of shrimp at a banquet marking the first graduation of rabbis from an American Jewish institution had a much deeper emotional impact on rabbis and ordinary Jews. It demonstrated decisively that the unity of the Union of American Hebrew Congregations was illusory, that Reform had taken the most serious steps, and that some counterreaction was necessary.

The counterreaction was led by Sabato Morais (1823–97), rabbi since 1851 of Mikveh Israel, the old Sephardic synagogue of Philadelphia, where he had succeeded Leeser. He had the support of the rabbis and laymen of about a dozen congregations. These included the three oldest synagogues of New York City and the oldest Ashkenazic synagogue of Philadelphia, whose rabbi was the distinguished scholar Marcus Jastrow (1829–1903). Under the leadership of Morais and with the important support of Congregation Shearith Israel's Rabbi Henry Pereira Mendes (1852–1937), a

Jewish Theological Seminary Association was formed in 1885 and began holding classes in the rooms of Congregation Shearith Israel in New York in 1887. The preamble to the constitution of the new association indicates clearly that its formation was a reaction to the radical position taken by Reform:

"The necessity has been made manifest for associated and organized effort on the part of the Jews of America faithful to Mosaic Law and ancestral traditions, for the purpose of keeping alive the true Judaic spirit; in particular by the establishment of a seminary where the Bible shall be impartially taught and rabbinical literature faithfully expounded, and more especially where youths, desirous of entering the ministry, may be thoroughly grounded in Jewish knowledge and inspired by the precept and example of their instructors with the love of the Hebrew language and a spirit of devotion and fidelity to the Jewish Law."[11]

A historian of the Conservative movement, Herbert Parzen, points out that of the eleven congregations that had supported the Jewish Theological Seminary in 1887, six had gone over to the Reform group by the end of the century. The seminary did not flourish. When Morais died in 1897, its future was in doubt. But meanwhile a completely new base for the support of such an institution had appeared in America. Alongside the few congregations opposing Reform, there were now hundreds of thousands of East European Jewish immigrants; the embattled leaders of Conservatism saw their opportunity. Henry Pereira Mendes, speaking after the death of Morais in 1897, asked, "Could he [Morais] foretell ten or twelve years ago that immense congregations would grow up in every city, faithful to so-called Orthodoxy but yet needing spiritual men, spiritual guides, who would be acceptable to them because loving what they love and honoring what they honor?"[12] In the new immigrants, whose Orthodoxy was of so unbending a nature that all the forms of Judaism in America, whether radical Reform, moderate Reform, or the dignified Orthodoxy of the old synagogues, seemed little better than heathenism— in these newcomers, the embattled representatives of tradition saw a new hope and a new means by which to stem the dominant stream of Reform.

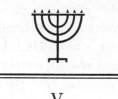

V

The East European Migration
1880-1920

In 1880 most of the approximately 250,000 Jews in America were identified with the synagogue, that is to say, with the Reform Temple. Most of them were immigrants or the descendants of immigrants from central Europe. By 1900 there had entered the country from eastern Europe some half-million immigrants who represented a completely different stage of culture and of Judaism. By the coming of the First World War, another million and a quarter had come into the country, and Reform was reduced, statistically, to the position of a denomination of high social level representing only a fraction of the American Jews.

It is most convenient to date the beginning of East European immigration from 1881/82, when a wave of pogroms and a series of new anti-Jewish decrees in Russia started a great tide of immigrants on the way to America. It was also in 1882 that societies to aid the immigrants sprang up in the leading European cities and in America, and that immigration became the chief problem of the American Jewish community. Of course, East European immigration to America had begun long before. There was already an East European congregation in New York City in 1852. All through the seventies, there was a fairly heavy immigration of East European Jews, which American Jewish newspapers discussed with concern. The year 1881, however, marks the beginning of large-scale mass immigration, which was to continue until the restrictive laws of the 1920's.

In Russia and Rumania, poverty and governmental anti-Semitism led many thousands every year to decide to go to America. In Galicia, part of Austria, poverty had the same effect. Before the First World War, the stream of immigration from eastern Europe had risen to one hundred thousand a year. These immigrants did not, like many of the contemporary immigrants from Italy and southeastern Europe, come to make their fortunes and return to the homeland. They did not consider Russia, Rumania, and Austria homelands. Exile was exile, and if America was a better place for making a living than Russia had been, fine, let it be America. They came with wives and children, and they came to stay.

The new immigrants were in many respects completely different from those who had come to these shores before. They came from a milieu in which they formed a very large part of the population and in which, in all-Jewish villages and towns, they had created a Jewish culture almost totally unaffected by the cultures of the people around them.

On their arrival in America, the East European Jews found a country in which the great westward expansion was coming to an end and in which the chief economic expansion of the future was to be in the cities. In response to this, the East European Jews did not spread out as the German Jews had done but tended to concentrate in the cities, where jobs were available, particularly in the rapidly developing clothing trades (in which, it is interesting to note, the entrepreneurs were largely German Jews). These East European Jews rapidly formed a proletariat in American cities, a working class, just as the East European Jews who were pouring into Lodz and Warsaw and Odessa formed a working class in those cities. It is in the light of this social background that we must consider the religious life and attitudes of the East European Jews.

In 1880 there were 270 synagogues in this country; by 1890 there were 533; by 1906, 1,769; and in 1916, 1,901. Almost all the new synagogues were those started by East European Jews, and there were perhaps scores or hundreds more that no census reached.

But figures cannot suggest the intensity of the Judaism of the East European Jews, which not only was unique in world history but represented something of a peak even in Jewish history. The East European Jews were attached to a religion that completely enveloped their lives and dictated a large part of their behavior. Among the immigrants were thousands of Jews with a fabulous knowledge of traditional law and usage, for the whole aim of Jewish life in eastern Europe was to produce students of the law. These congregations had no need for rabbis, let alone "ministers": even the most ignorant knew the Hebrew text of the prayers and the melodies that traditionally accompanied them, and the whole congregation formed a spontaneous if discordant choir. Each congregation had dozens of men who knew the prayers well enough to lead it.

But this was only half the picture of the spiritual life of the East European Jews. For they too had been to some extent affected by contemporary thought, by rational philosophy, modern science, and contemporary radical social movements. In Germany, the effect of the modern world on the Jews had been to lead many to conversion and assimilation and others to create Reform Judaism. In eastern Europe, its effect was quite different. The East European Jews did not convert in any significant numbers, they did not assimilate, and they did not attempt to transform the traditional religion. The first impact of the Enlightenment, of Western ideas in brief, on the East European Jew led to a movement to create a modernized Hebrew tongue, which could be used for the political and cultural uplift of the masses. In time, the new ideas from the West led to the rise of powerful nationalist (Zionist and non-Zionist) and socialist movements: none of them had any place for religion, traditional or reformed.

It is worth considering why it is that the impact of the Enlightenment on German Jewry created Reform, while the Enlightenment in eastern Europe created radical, antireligious movements. There seem to have been two reasons. For one, traditional Judaism was far stronger in eastern Europe in the late nineteenth century than it had been in Germany in the early years of the century. East European Jewish life was remarkable, even in Jewish history, for the single-mindedness with which it pursued the study of the Jewish law and banned every other form of education as heretical. Everything about the law became holy; even the fact that Yiddish was used to expound the Talmud gave that language a kind of holy character, and it became unthinkable that the Talmud might be expounded in Russian or German or English. No rabbi broke with traditional Judaism to lead or demand something like German Reform in eastern Europe; the prospect would have struck him as so hopeless that he would have decided rather, as many did, to abandon any ideas of religious leadership. In Germany, by contrast, traditional Judaism had already moved by the early nineteenth century some distance from its most extreme forms, and there were not only rabbis to lead reforms but many in the middle group who gave the reformers partial support.

Perhaps more important than this were the differences between German and eastern European society. The Jews of Germany lived in an ethnically homogeneous society which was attempting to become a modern national state. They could envisage themselves becoming a religion, like the Lutherans or Roman Catholics, and enjoying all the benefits of full citizenship and perhaps even social equality; only their peculiar customs, they thought, stood in their way. In eastern Europe, it was impossible to think this way. The countries of eastern Europe were not ethnically homogeneous and religiously diverse as was Germany. They were composed of many national groups, some struggling to free themselves from the oppression of others. Religion tended to be intimately tied up with nationality: the Poles were Catholic; the Russians, Greek Orthodox; the German enclaves, Protestant; and so on. In such a situation, the Jews, and the non-Jews too, naturally thought of the Jews as a nation, for that is what they were in eastern Europe. It was easier to envisage the Jews abandoning their religion and becoming simply a people than to envisage them abandoning their ethnic characteristics and becoming a denomination in Reform Jewish style. East European Jews thought of the problems they faced in *national* terms, and the main point of Reform Judaism, that the Jews were, or would become, a religion, appeared meaningless to them, and indeed, in eastern European terms, it was meaningless.

We must now add that not only were ethnic characteristics and religion linked in Europe but both were linked with class, which again distinguished eastern Europe from Germany. In Germany, the Jewish middle class paralleled a German middle class, using the same language, having the same cultural attributes, and differing, it would seem, only in religion. It was reasonable for German Jews to think that Reform Judaism, in modifying these differences of religion, would enable them to become an accepted part of the German middle class and, consequently, of the German nation. Just as the German middle class had its dignified services, its hymns, its preachers, and its schools teaching morality, so too would the Jews.

The East European Migration

In eastern Europe the situation was entirely different. When the Enlightenment began to make an impact, the Jews were, it is true, largely middle-class traders, shopkeepers, and the like. But the ferocious anti-Semitism of populace and government was rapidly transforming them into a proletariat. Even for the Jews who were not becoming workers, the German parallel did not hold; for there was no model of a modern middle class to which middle-class Jews could aspire. During the late nineteenth century, the industrial revolution came to western Russia; cities grew, and there did arise an important non-Jewish middle class. But this non-Jewish middle class consisted largely of a state bureaucracy from which Jews were banned and which was so anti-Semitic that it would have been fantastic for the Jews as a group to think of becoming integrated into it by modifying their religious practices.

For all these reasons, socialism, anarchism, Zionism, and other radical secular political movements flourished among the East European Jews, particularly among those who moved to the cities from the small towns. There were Zionist socialists who wanted to set up a socialist state in Palestine; national socialists who wanted socialism with minority rights for the Jews in eastern Europe; and antinational socialists who simply wanted socialism and assumed, following Marx, that the Jews, as a decadent caste of merchants tied to capitalism, would disappear once socialism was established. Then there were Zionists of various persuasions: those who were socialists, those who were religious, those who wanted a Jewish state because it would revive Jewish culture, and those who simply wanted a Jewish state in Israel and did not care about religion one way or another. Then there were the Diaspora nationalists, those who wanted to see the Jews legally established as a separate nation with rights as a minority in Europe. And there were the territorialists who wanted to establish a state anywhere, and there were those who simply wanted to assimilate. Not all these positions were to be found in eastern Europe as early as the 1880's, of course; forty years later they had all appeared in one way or another.

There were thus a number of proposed solutions to the Jewish problem among the immigrants from eastern Europe, but none of these was Reform Judaism. Reform Jews, to the masses of the Orthodox immigrants, were scarcely better than Gentiles; to the masses of politically radical and secular-minded immigrants, Reform Jews, whatever their formal position on social justice, were simply bourgeois hypocrites and exploiters.

To the established, middle-class, Americanized German Jews of the 1880's, the East European immigrants were a frightening apparition. Their poverty was more desperate than German Jewish poverty, their piety more intense than German Jewish piety, their irreligion more violent than German Jewish irreligion, their radicalism more extreme than German Jewish radicalism. It is not surprising that the American Jews viewed this immigration, initially, with mixed feelings, and some even suggested the possibility of deflecting or preventing it. In 1884, according to Irving Aaron Mandel's study of the Jewish press in this period, "the State of New York had passed restrictive immigration laws, and *The American Israelite* [edited by Isaac Mayer Wise] suggested the use of these laws by the immigration authorities to return some 200 indigent Russian refugees who were about to arrive on the steamer 'California' "![1]

By the 1890's these feelings had been largely overcome, at least among the leaders of the Jewish community. In part, Mandel suggests, the great outpouring of sympathy for the immigrants by the American press influenced the Jewish leaders to take a more kindly point of view. But in any case, even from the beginning, we find the established Jewish community, despite its very clear indications of distaste, coming to the aid of the immigrants: establishing organizations to help them, setting up schools and lecture courses, and trying, often ill-advisedly, to "uplift" them. The tendency of these efforts may be indicated by the suggestion of the editor of the *Jewish Messenger* in New York that the East European Jews needed someone who would teach them to distinguish "the Judaism of an Isaiah and of an obscure cabbalistical Maggid."[2]

The American Jews of the period did not know whether to object most to the Orthodoxy of the immigrants, which was as distasteful to the old, dignified Orthodox synagogues that opposed Reform as it was to the Reform synagogues, or to the radicalism of the immigrants. For from the beginning the immigrants showed both traits. There were enough of them to create a flourishing and intense religious life, as well as a flourishing and intense life in the radical political organizations and unions. Just how many of the immigrants adhered to one point of view and how many to the other is hard to say. It is perhaps most accurate to conceive of them as forming a continuum, with the religious Jews at one end, the most radical at the other, and many in the middle who were both religious and radical in varying degrees. It was not uncommon for a Jewish worker to read an antireligious Yiddish newspaper, vote Socialist, join a socialist union, and yet attend the synagogue weekly, or even daily, and observe most of the Jewish law.

But whatever the proportions of the religious and radical elements among the immigrants to begin with, there is no question that the impact of America (as indeed of the large cities of eastern Europe) was to reduce the number of the Orthodox and increase the number of the radical. Once again, as in Germany in the early nineteenth century, it was demonstrated how little staying power traditional Judaism had when it came in contact with the modern world.

If one had to select a single person to epitomize the German

Jewish immigration, it would be Isaac Mayer Wise. And if one had to select a single person to stand for East European Jews in America, it would be Abraham Cahan, the editor of the *Jewish Daily Forward*. Cahan, born near Vilna in 1860, had received the Orthodox elementary education of eastern Europe. With a passion for a modern education, he had gone on to be educated in a Russian government school, which, while intensely Jewish and religious, as was any institution that hoped to make any impact on East European Jews, was also modern in the sense that the curriculum was not restricted to rabbinic literature. As a young man Cahan was attracted to the Jewish radical groups of Vilna, who thought of themselves as Russian and used the Russian language. He emigrated to America in 1882. He had hoped to become a Russian writer and had learned the language well. In America he immediately set about learning English, which he mastered so thoroughly that he became a reporter for the New York newspaper edited by Lincoln Steffens and wrote novels of immigrant Jewish life that were praised by William Dean Howells.

Cahan was drawn into the activities of the radical groups in New York and soon learned that if he hoped to have any influence on the immigrant Jewish population, he would have to address them, not in Russian, the language of the radical Russian Jewish intellectuals, and not in English, but in Yiddish. Just as Wise, to influence the German Jews of the 1850's, had to establish a German newspaper despite his strong feeling of the desirability of Americanization, so Cahan, to influence the Jewish masses of the 1890's, became a Yiddish newspaper editor and established what was eventually to become the largest Yiddish daily. Cahan was also an Americanizer. He was a socialist, but one who kept emphasizing the need to know America, and he attacked the theorists who acted in America just as they would have acted in Russia. Cahan's pri-

mary interest, one feels, was not socialism per se but the transforming of Jewish immigrants into modern citizens. In Cahan's
day, it was impossible for a dynamic transforming element to
emerge from a Judaism that seemed irrelevant to the modern
world, and Cahan therefore had nothing to do with religion.
He expressed impulses similar to those which had moved Wise
in his time by creating a daily newspaper to instruct, uplift, and
Americanize the immigrant Europeans.

In one of his novels, the best yet written about American Jewish
life, we are given a vivid and convincing picture of the helplessness
and irrelevance of East European Judaism in the America of the
early years of the mass immigration. We read in *The Rise of David
Levinsky* of how a young Russian Jewish yeshiva student, learned
and pious, emigrates to this country. On the boat he eats no forbidden food and prays daily. In America he seeks out and finds
solace in the synagogue established by the people from his home
town. But he also moves inevitably from one transgression to the
next. First his earlocks are cut off, then he shaves, soon he abandons
the synagogue in favor of night school and English studies. And
soon nothing is left—and with practically no soul-searching.

The case of David Levinsky illustrates the crucial point that
Judaism in eastern Europe, as in Germany, tended to ignore everything that might be considered theology. Only the practices of Judaism were taught. One was brought up to observe the commandments, and, for this reason, as soon as one came in touch with a
kind of thought which questioned fundamentals, one was at a loss.
In other words, it may be said Jews lost their faith so easily because
they had no faith to lose: that is, they had no doctrine, no collection
of dogmas to which they could cling and with which they could
resist argument. All they had, surrounding them like an armor, was
a complete set of practices, each presumably as holy as the next.

Once this armor was pierced by the simple question, Why? it fell away, and all that was left was a collection of habits. Not that these habits could be dismissed completely. In some cases these were enough to supply the individual with a repertory of religious observances of a variety and complexity that would put the piety of any Christian to shame. A non-believing Jew might still, from habit, observe the dietary laws, go to synagogue now and then (and when he went, so thorough was the East European training, he often knew most of the prayers by heart), say Kaddish (a memorial prayer) for his father, and so on.

At the beginning, the religious elements among the new immigrants thought of re-establishing in America the kind of religious organization they were familiar with in eastern Europe, in which a central community organized religious life, and the synagogue was under the authority of the community. In 1888, the leading synagogues of the East European Jews in New York co-operated in bringing to this country as a chief rabbi Jacob Joseph, a well-known scholar and the communal preacher of Vilna. There were then 130 synagogues for East European Jews in New York, and only a small part of them were involved in this enterprise. Almost immediately, the antagonism of the non-co-operating synagogues, the violent attacks of radical Jews, the opposition or indifference of the "uptown" elements, and the misguided effort to support the chief rabbi's office by a tax on kosher products brought the enterprise to an unhappy conclusion. The congregational independence of the East European Orthodox synagogues remained unhampered by any powerful central organization.

We have seen why it was inconceivable for the Reform Judaism of the American Jews or, for that matter, that of the few dignified Orthodox synagogues to have any impact on the East European Jews. The significant impact on the traditional religion of this group was made not by religious alternatives but by secular ones, that is, the movements of secular salvation—socialism, anarchism, and Zionism.

Zionism was rather less influential among the Jewish East European immigrants than radicalism. As against socialism and anarchism, however, Zionism tended to bring some of the East European Jews into contact with the older American Jewish community. For important figures, rabbis and laymen, in the American Jewish community were also Zionists. Indeed, the rabbi of Temple Emanuel, Gustav Gottheil (1827–1903), and his son, Richard (1862–1936), together with Stephen S. Wise (1874–1949), Benjamin Szold (1829–1902), and other leaders of the long-settled American Jewish community, were active Zionists and leaders of the American affiliate of the world-wide Zionist organization established by Theodor Herzl. But in this context the important thing to note is that the Zionism of the 1890's and later decades in Europe and America tended to disintegrate traditional East European Orthodoxy almost as thoroughly as did socialism and anarchism. It too was largely a secular, Western movement, indifferent to the central concern of Judaism, the maintenance and teaching of the Jewish law.

And on this central ground, the religion of the immigrants was in steady retreat. They made heroic efforts to re-create in America the elaborate system of religious education by which they had produced a steady stream of prodigies of rabbinic learning in Europe. The established American Jewish community offered no model for Jewish education. Following the collapse of the synagogue schools of the 1850's under competition from the public schools, the established synagogues of New York had limited themselves to Sunday or Sabbath schools, meeting one or two days a week. The schools that the German Jews set up to help Americanize the immigrants were, from the point of view of the East European Jews, totally inadequate for the purposes of education, even though these schools conducted a far more intensive religious education than their German Jewish patrons gave to their own children.

The East European Jews resorted for the most part to private teachers who generally set up tiny schools in single rooms where they taught what they could of Hebrew, the prayer book, and the Bible to an unruly group of children. These *heders* were looked upon with horror by the settled Jewish community. There were also some rather more professional schools, Talmud Torahs, which had a number of classrooms and graded classes, and were supported by tuition fees and the contributions of both East European Jews and some of the more broad-minded German Jews. Some of these institutions grew into large and excellent schools, conducted after public-school hours, supported by the Jewish community as a whole, and offering an intelligent précis of the traditional education of eastern Europe. In 1887 a full-time elementary school, the Etz-Chaim Talmudical Academy, was founded in New York to teach the traditional curriculum of the East European schools. In 1896 the Rabbi Isaac Elchanan Theological Seminary, the first yeshiva in America (the yeshiva is the higher school of the East European system) was established in New York. In 1915 the two merged. The head of the new institution was Bernard Revel (1885–1940), and under his administration it was to grow into present-day Yeshiva University. It is suggestive of conditions in the Orthodox group in 1915 that Revel was only part-time head of the new institution at first and did not, we are informed by an official historian, withdraw wholly from "commercial activities" until 1921.[3]

All these efforts reached only a small proportion of the children of the immigrants. In 1908, when there were about 1,800,000 Jews in the United States, of whom probably three-quarters were East European immigrants and their children, it was estimated that only 28 per cent of the Jewish children of school age were receiving any form of education, and a quarter of these were in the almost useless Sunday schools. In 1910, only about a fifth of the Jewish children of school age in New York City were receiving any Jewish education. Of course there was a pattern whereby children attended Jewish *hadarim* and other schools for only a few years, so that for any given generation considerably more would have attended some sort of school or been exposed to some religious education.

But in any case, it was naïve to think that education could check the flight of the children from East European Orthodoxy. Those who had the best Talmud-Torah education were as likely to drop all religious observances in late adolescence or early adulthood as those who had received none. The hundreds and thousands of synagogues organized by the East European Jews were the work of the immigrants themselves; the children had no part in them and wished none. The rate of attrition was so rapid that it seemed two generations would end East European Orthodoxy.

As I have said, the established Jewish community was worried by both the Orthodoxy and the radicalism of the East European Jews. And they saw the two as connected: finding the Orthodoxy repellent, one popular theory went, the East European Jewish youth abandoned all religion and became radical. While this cause-and-effect theory was oversimplified, it did suggest a course of action to some leaders of the established Jewish community. For example, Henry Pereira Mendes, speaking ten years after the Jewish Theological Seminary had been established by the older, Conservative American congregations, described the problem of the East European congregations thus: "We have to choose between striving for learning and culture or allow these communities to honor learning of but one kind in their own peculiar way, to maintain services which show little love of culture and which repel, methods which fail in the second generation."[4]

One very important motive in the German Jews' efforts to

Americanize the East European Jews was the feeling that the crude religion as well as the extreme radicalism of the Jewish immigrants might affect their own solid middle-class position. The coming of the East European Jews, they believed, had adversely affected the social position of the upper-class Jewish families in New York. After all, were they not all Jews, Germans and East Europeans alike, and would not the ordinary American, who cared little for fine distinctions, think of all Jews as crude and radical?

But again, the efforts of the American Jewish leaders had a broader motivation than this. The established Jewish community had a certain disinterested concern for fellow Jews. They saw themselves as lifting the East European Jews out of superstition into light.

Perhaps in the best position to do something about the matter were those few congregations and their leaders who remained close to traditional Judaism, who still upheld the authority of the religious law, and who, at least on the ground of formal creed, were related to the East European Jews. This was the group that had established the Jewish Theological Seminary (see pp. 58–60) and that saw it slowly dying in the late nineties. What now happened was that the Seminary, whose original base of traditional synagogues had been slowly shrinking, was reorganized and given the function of ministering to and civilizing the great new East European masses. This delicate operation was performed largely by Cyrus Adler (1863–1940), who held a most important position in the Jewish life of the times. Adler had been born in a small town in Arkansas and had been raised in Philadelphia by a widowed mother who came from an important German Jewish family, the Sulzbergers. Through the Sulzbergers, Adler was related to or knew important figures in the German Jewish community. He was also a pupil of Sabato Morais of Mikveh Israel, the old Sephardic synagogue of Philadelphia, and he became a figure in the dignified Orthodox circles of Philadelphia and New York. In 1887 Adler was appointed to the department of Semitics of the Johns Hopkins University, and in 1892 he became assistant secretary of the Smithsonian Institution. He had a vast acquaintanceship among Jews and non-Jews in this country and abroad, among scholars, businessmen, politicians, and philanthropists.

Adler saw that the Jewish Theological Seminary might serve to turn young East European Jews into modern, English-speaking rabbis for the East European Orthodox masses. Certainly the Reform Hebrew Union College could not do this; at the other extreme, the schools of the East Europeans themselves were conducted as if they were located in Russia or Poland.

In 1901 Adler suggested to Jacob Schiff (1847–1920) that he and his friends put up the money to restore the Jewish Theological Seminary, then inactive, on an expanded scale. Schiff himself was an interesting figure. From a distinguished Jewish family of Frankfurt, he came to America at the age of eighteen and became a partner of Kuhn, Loeb and Company. He had a good Jewish education, wide interests, and showed a remarkable capacity for spreading his money about to great effect, even though the sums were often not large. Schiff himself was a Reform Jew, but with his knowledge of the Jewish tradition, he looked with more sympathy upon the Jews from eastern Europe than did many of his fellow Reform Jews. Schiff, together with Daniel and Simon Guggenheim, Leonard Lewissohn, Mayer Sulzberger, Louis Marshall, and others, soon collected a fund of half a million dollars for the Seminary and thus made it possible to bring from England Solomon Schechter (1847–1915) as its new president.

Solomon Schechter was a great Jewish scholar who had in 1896 recognized on a scrap of paper the Hebrew of the apocryphal book of Ecclesiasticus and in 1897 discovered a great hoard of ancient Hebrew manuscripts in Cairo. He was also reader in Rabbinics at Cambridge University in England. He was an East European Jew who, like so many brilliant Talmudic students, had migrated to central Europe for a secular education. With his East European background and his experience in England, he was the perfect man to head the new institution and to mediate between the Reform Jews who sat on the board of directors and the East European Jews who came to be trained as rabbis in the Western mode.

Schechter's view of Judaism was quite different from that of either Reform or traditional Orthodoxy. He had a very strong attachment to all varieties of Judaism and was appreciative of the minor streams of mysticism as well as the major stream of legal development. A thoroughly competent Western scholar, he had nevertheless not acquired from his German teachers the disdain for the religion of the East Europeans characteristic of many German Jewish scholars, devotees of the Wissenschaft des Judentums. Schechter was also a Zionist, as against Schiff, Marshall, and other members of the board of directors, as well as Cyrus Adler. Schechter saw that the Orthodoxy of the immigrants was dying and hoped that it could be revived in the form of a rather more dignified Orthodoxy. The word "decorum," heard so often in the Reform discussions of the previous century, was again heard, now from Schechter.

Despite his deep love of every strand of Judaism and Jewishness, Schechter was in other ways an heir of the Reform movement, for he had a great faith in and devotion to modern scholarship. In theory he accepted the idea that Judaism would change in response to modern conditions, but he saw these changes as controlled by a scholarship which would discover what was essential to Judaism and which could guide and set a limit to change. Just how this was to be done was never very clear, for it is never easy to go from the "is" (or rather "was") to the "ought." Schechter also felt that the Hebrew Bible was being threatened by the higher criticism of the German scholars and believed that the Jews needed their own scholars to defend it.

Impelled by his commitment to scholarship, Schechter gathered together a faculty of great scholars, East European and German Jews of Orthodox background but with training in the German universities. He set up a school to train traditional rabbis who could speak English and stay abreast of modern scholarship. And good numbers of young East European Jews came to the institution with their previously acquired learning in rabbinic literature to receive the finishing it offered. They then took not typical East European congregations but, rather, congregations made up of Jews who had been here some time and were still fairly conservative. Initially, the Seminary had little influence on the East European Jews, aside from offering an avenue of upward social mobility to some of its young men. But in time the number of Conservative synagogues, as they were called, for they were neither Reform nor East European Orthodox, grew, and in 1913 Schechter collected sixteen of them to form the United Synagogue of America, an organization of synagogues designed to oppose the older, much larger, and more powerful group of Reform synagogues, the Union of American Hebrew Congregations. In 1915 Schechter died, and Cyrus Adler, who was already president of Dropsie College, a new graduate school in Philadelphia for studies in Hebrew and related subjects, succeeded him as president of the Seminary and the United Synagogue of America.

The Seminary was one means by which the older element of the American Jewish community tried to affect the religious life of the East European Jews. Another such effort was much less successful.

In 1898, when the Seminary was at the low point in its history following the death of Sabato Morais, Rabbi Mendes of Shearith Israel, trying to strengthen the Conservative element by allying it to the great numbers of East European Jews, founded the Union of Orthodox Jewish Congregations. The East European congregations soon ran away with the organization, which still exists as the central body of the larger Orthodox congregations, and refused to recognize the Seminary as possessing the authority to ordain rabbis. After all, the Seminary was no European yeshiva, and it was inconceivable to most East European rabbis that a man who studied the Talmud in English rather than in Yiddish could be a real rabbi.

In 1902, the East European Orthodox rabbis organized their own rabbinical group, the Union of Orthodox Rabbis. (This, too, still exists, but by now the English-speaking Orthodox rabbis have their own organization.) The majority of the congregations and rabbis of the East European immigrants joined neither group, and there was no institution to serve as a center for the religious life of the East European Jew.

Aside from the distinguished lay figures we have mentioned—Schiff, Marshall, and others—Reform had little to do with the East European Jews. Its main institutions, its college and its congregational union, were located in Cincinnati, far from New York. After about 1900, Reform grew slowly; it had already swept up almost every German Jewish congregation in the country. It was remarkably distant from the Judaism of the East European Jews, and there seemed to be no way of making contact. But, as we shall see, even Reform Judaism was affected, at first in subtle ways, and later more directly, by the great East European immigration.

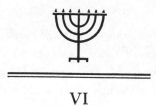

VI

Judaism and Jewishness
1920–45

The dividing lines of history are seldom clear; but in the third decade of the present century falls one of the most decisive dates in the history of Jews in America. In the period between 1900 and 1914, immigration into this country reached its peak, and Jewish immigration was greater than ever before. The First World War stopped the immigration for four years. It resumed in a huge flood after the war, a flood made up largely of Jews escaping from a bolshevized Russia and the ravaged, economically depressed, and anti-Semitic new states of eastern Europe. But, in the meantime, much had changed in America. The agitation against immigration, which had generally been conducted by the less educated part of the population (including many recent immigrants) against the insistence of a more enlightened upper class, now became more and more powerful. The Johnson Act, imposing quotas on immigration, became law in 1921, and a more stringent system of quotas was imposed in 1924, bringing mass immigration to an end. In that year, fifty thousand Jews entered the country; in the next, ten thousand.

The immigration had meant a continual and heavy renewal of the East European element in the Jewish population, so that the picture of the American Jews in the 1920's had much in common with that in the 1890's. Of course, there were changes in the areas of Europe from which the immigrants came, and the later immigrants tended to be perhaps less Orthodox than the earlier. But the major characteristics remained the same. All through this period, the immigrants were either impoverished traders or artisans or factory workers. On arrival, they usually became workers in the large eastern cities. Ideologically they were divided between Jews who were extremely religious and those who had taken up one of the modern secular outlooks, principally socialism.

But all Jews, even workers, showed the effects of a two-thousand-year-old experience as merchants and scholars. The Jewish working class had a broader horizon than the working class of other groups. They tended to form powerful unions, which helped improve their conditions. And they made sure their children would not also be workers. As early as 1900, so authoritative a historian of the American working classes as John R. Commons observed that "Jewish women are employed [in factories] to a much less extent than the women of other nationalities, and their children are kept in school until 15 or 16 years of age. It is quite unusual for Jewish tailors to teach their children their own trade."[1] With the Jewish mother at home, the Jewish child received a better education and better care, as shown in lower delinquency and death rates. The Jewish child, strongly urged on by his working-class parents, was a prodigy in school. Another authoritative observer in 1900 wrote, in the report of the Industrial Commission of that year, "In the lower schools, the Jewish children are the delight of their teachers for cleverness at their books, obedience, and general good conduct."[2] Never were teachers in slum schools happier than when they had Jewish pupils; never were settlement-house workers more delighted with the results of their work than when the Jews filled the slums of the large cities.

Judaism and Jewishness

By 1908 a government report showed that 8.5 per cent of the male student body of seventy-seven major institutions of higher learning were composed of first- and second-generation Jews. (Jews at this time made up about 2 per cent of the population.) And in that year, the same report showed that one-third of the Jewish immigrants were already in trade (mostly small, retail businesses). Of course most of the immigrants remained workers. Their children, however, were being prepared by the intensive education that was characteristic of the Jewish immigrants for a phenomenal advance in their social position. During the period between 1920 and 1940 a great social change was under way which would transform a community that was largely made up of workers into one that is today largely made up of middle-class people: white-collar workers, businessmen, and professionals. Initially masked by the arrival of large, new, working-class elements, the change was further delayed by the great depression of the thirties. But it was being prepared by intense education and by significant shifts in occupations.

One of the most striking manifestations of this coming change, which was of great consequence for the Jewish religion, was the desertion, during the twenties, of the areas of first settlement, the teeming city districts in which the immigrants had settled and raised their children. As the prosperity of the First World War and then of the twenties affected the Jews, workers and small store-keepers alike, they deserted the areas of first settlement for new city districts. Thus the Lower East Side of New York City, which held 353,000 Jews in 1916, held only 121,000 in 1930. The old "ghetto" area of Chicago lost half its Jewish population between 1914 and 1920. The same thing happened in Boston, Philadelphia, Baltimore, and the other major centers of Jewish population. As a result of this migration, the division of the Jewish community into an "uptown," long-settled German-Jewish group and a "downtown," newly arrived East European Jewish group was modified drastically. The East European Jews now moved uptown, and the uptown Jews either remained to form a mixed community in which the lines between the two groups became less sharp or moved on outward to areas of "third settlement." In this period, then, we can visualize the Jewish communities of America as made up of rapidly emptying areas of first settlement (slums), of rapidly growing areas of second settlement (middle-class apartment houses or two-family houses or, least frequently, single-family dwellings), and areas of third settlement (expensive apartment-house areas or suburban developments of single-family houses).

The East European Jewish community was divided in this period between a first generation of needle-trades workers, small shopkeepers, and small businessmen, some of whom had become quite wealthy, and a second generation of high-school- and college-educated children, most of whom were working at some white-collar occupation—as bookkeepers, accountants, salesmen, clerks, and the like. Many of them were in business or considering entering business and were being held back by the great depression, and a rapidly increasing number of them were becoming professionals. The effect of this great interest of the immigrants' children in the professions shows up strikingly in studies of Jewish communities conducted in the thirties. Thus, in San Francisco, eighteen out of every thousand gainfully employed Jews were lawyers or judges, sixteen were doctors (among non-Jews, five out of every thousand were lawyers and judges; the same number, doctors). In Pittsburgh, fourteen out of every thousand gainfully employed Jews were lawyers or judges, thirteen were doctors (among non-Jews, the figures for each of these occupations was four).

In 1917, it was estimated that there were about 3,400,000 Jews in the country and that they formed about 3.3 per cent of the American population. In 1927, it was estimated that about eight hundred thousand had been added by immigration and natural increase and that the Jews formed perhaps 3.6 per cent of the population. After that year, the Jewish proportion of the American population became fixed or, if anything, decreased, for with only a trickle of immigrants and with a rapidly declining birth rate, reflecting both the extreme urbanization and the rising social status of most Jews, the natural increase of the Jewish population lagged behind that of the population as a whole.

The Jews of America by 1927 were probably 80 per cent or more of East European origin. In the big cities this proportion was even higher. As one moved away from the greatest centers of Jewish concentration, one found communities in which the German Jews formed a larger part of the population. In general, the German Jews had been more evenly spread about the country. And in general, as a reflection both of the geographic distribution of German Jews and East European Jews and of the simple facts of opportunity, the proportion of manual workers in Jewish communities dropped as one went from large to small cities and towns and villages. In the smallest Jewish communities and even in those of only two or three thousand Jews, almost everyone was either a shopkeeper, an entrepreneur, or in the professions.

The religious situation reflected these circumstances. The original stronghold of Orthodoxy had been the "ghettos" of the large cities. In New York City the ghetto areas, even after the emigrations of the twenties, still contained thousands of Jews. By a process of cultural as well as economic selection, those who remained behind were not only the poorer Jews but also the more religious ones. So religion, in its almost unadulterated East European form, still flourished in these reduced ghetto areas. There one could still buy kosher food at every street corner, eat in kosher restaurants, and send one's children to religious schools that met in the afternoon or to all-day schools in which a part of the curriculum was devoted to English studies, to fulfil the requirements of state law. In these areas there were synagogues to meet every variant of Orthodox need: Ashkenazic and Sephardic, Hasidic and Misnagdic (the Hasidim are adherents of an enthusiastic-mystical tendency in Judaism; the Misnagdim are their opponents), Lithuanian and Galician, Polish, Russian, Rumanian, Hungarian, and subvariants of each. Here too were published the Yiddish newspapers and magazines, the Hebrew newspapers and magazines, the Yiddish and Hebrew books. There were so many Jews in America that, despite the statistical trends, there were in absolute numbers enough Orthodox Jews to keep up a flourishing religious life.

In the areas of second settlement in the big cities, the predominant type of synagogue was still Orthodox, generally of a slightly modified form. It was larger, more formal, and the sermons were in English. There would also be synagogues in which these changes had gone so far that they called themselves "Conservative" and an example here and there of a Reform temple, left over from the days when the neighborhood was made up of German Jews, or perhaps newly organized by a group of more Americanized East European Jews. In the areas of third settlement, that is, in the upper-class residential neighborhoods of the large cities and among the well-to-do of the smaller ones, Reform temples were predominant, but Conservative synagogues competed with them. Among the well-to-do Jews the Orthodox were a very small minority. In the smaller cities and towns, where social movements were somewhat abbreviated, the areas of second and third settlement tended to be indistinct.

In the years between 1920 and 1940, the areas of second settlement contained the greatest number of American Jews, and it was in this zone of American Jewish life that the pattern of the future was being developed. The future, it then seemed, would see the rapid dissolution of the Jewish religion. True, the number of congregations, synagogues, and synagogue buildings continued to grow. In 1927 there were thirty-one hundred congregations; in 1937, thirty-seven hundred. The number of synagogue buildings rose by more than one thousand (from 1,782 to 2,851). All through the twenties elaborate synagogues were built, and for the first time the synagogue as a large communal structure, containing classrooms, gymnasiums, and auditoriums, became common. Jewish institutions were not weak. Indeed, fund-raising became more systematic and "scientific," and institutions of all kinds, including religious institutions, became more secure. But while all these material advances could be pointed out, it was nevertheless true that the overwhelming majority of the immigrants' children had deserted Judaism. They did not convert, but they were either indifferent or hostile to the traditional religion. In 1935, to cite one striking fact, a survey was made of the youth of New York City, in which every tenth person between the ages of fifteen and twenty-five was interviewed. Among other things, they were asked about their attendance at religious services. Seventy-two per cent of the young Jewish men and 78 per cent of the young Jewish women had attended no religious service at all during the past year. Eighty-nine per cent of the young men and 94 per cent of the young women had attended no service during the past week. All during the twenties and thirties studies were made on various campuses of the religious beliefs of college students. Again and again it was discovered that the Jewish students had moved much farther from any religious position than the Catholic and Protestant students. More were atheist, more agnostic, fewer accepted any traditional religious formulations. By simple extrapolation, it seemed inconceivable that such a generation could or would maintain the thirty-seven hundred congregations that served American Jewry.

And yet, Jewish education, like all of Jewish life, was much better organized in this period than at any time before. The week-day school, which taught Jewish history, Hebrew, the reading of the prayer book, and the like, became quite popular. Sometimes it was communally maintained; sometimes it was attached to the synagogue. In any case, the day when all Jewish religious education consisted of the Sunday school had passed. Ironically enough, it had been the Hebrew Free School Association, set up in 1864 by uptown New York Jews to help downtown New York Jews (more specifically, to keep them from attending schools conducted by Christian missionaries), that had been the first major example of the weekday school. Later the incoming East European immigrants adapted the *heder* to the needs of a society in which all the children went to public school. Finally, in the twenties and thirties, afternoon schools, private, congregational, and communal, became a major form of Jewish education. In 1935 it was estimated that about one-quarter of the Jewish children of school age were receiving some kind of Jewish education, more than half of them in the weekday schools. Probably two-thirds or three-quarters of the Jewish children received some Jewish education at some point in their school years. A tiny fraction, three thousand children in all, attended all-day schools (all Orthodox), which offered an intensive Jewish education.

But this Jewish education often had nothing to do with the Jewish religion, just as the very active Jewish life of the concentrated communities of Jews in the areas of second settlement did not necessarily have anything to do with the Jewish religion. For, as I have pointed out, the Jewish religion or Judaism was only one of a number of contending influences in the Jewish community. Thus, many of the schools that Jewish children attended after public school were not only neutral toward religion but were on principle atheistic and antireligious. This was the case with a good part of the very active

Yiddish school movement. Just as the passage of time, the arrival of new immigrants, and growing competence in adapting to the American scene had strengthened the institutions of Judaism, so had it strengthened the institutions of Jewish socialism, which were particularly attached to Yiddish, the language of the Jewish masses. And this attachment was encouraged by the fact that the "bourgeois" and "chauvinistic" Zionists naturally favored the Hebrew language. In 1910 the first Yiddish school system was launched by the Zionist socialists, who, though Zionists, supported Yiddish as the language of the Jewish masses. In 1916 the Workmen's Circle, a large and important socialist and anti-Zionist organization, also began to organize Yiddish schools. It was only natural that, in opposition to these party schools, a non-political school system, the Sholem Aleichem schools, should have been established. When the Communists split from all the socialist organizations after the First World War, they established their own Yiddish schools. These were the major groups of non- or antireligious Yiddish schools. In the mid-thirties seven thousand New York City children attended these schools.

In describing the Yiddish school systems, we have referred to only the merest fraction of the active non-religious Jewish life of the period. Socialists, Communists, anarchists, Zionists of all types, territorialists (those who wanted a Jewish state, but not in Palestine), and combinations of them all, in the dense areas of Jewish settlement in the big cities, had their groups, their centers, their social events, their newspapers and periodicals. Outside of politics there were the cultural Yiddishists and Hebraists with their circles and centers, their publishing organizations, and newspapers and magazines.

On a somewhat higher social level, there were other forms of Jewish life which had little or nothing to do with the Jewish religion. These were the philanthropic, defense, and benevolent societies. The German Jews had organized B'nai B'rith, a fraternal organization, in 1845. In time, this organization lost its German Jewish cast to become the major middle-class men's organization in the Jewish community. The son of a socialist worker would himself very likely, if he were a business or professional man, become a member of B'nai B'rith. In 1913, the organization formed the Anti-Defamation League, in which many of its members became active in the fight against anti-Semitism. In the twenties and thirties, anti-Semitism was to become a major concern of the Jewish community.

B'nai B'rith had been preceded in this work by the American Jewish Committee. The latter organization had been founded in 1906 by very much the same group that had come to the support of the Jewish Theological Seminary—Schiff, Adler, Marshall, and Mayer Sulzberger were the major figures—to defend the rights of Jews everywhere. It remained a relatively small though influential body and did not reach out for members beyond the German Jewish community until the forties. In 1929, Cyrus Adler added the presidency of the American Jewish Committee to the other presidencies he filled. The committee, while it did not affect any very large number of American Jews directly, again illustrates the pattern whereby major functions of Jewish life were conducted independently of organized religion.

Most significant in this respect were the philanthropic organizations. In every major Jewish community there were Jewish hospitals, orphanages, old people's homes, settlement houses, social agencies for the poor. Many well-to-do Jews spent a good part of their lives administering and raising money for these organizations and the central fund-raising bodies that assisted them. Then there were the major fund-raising bodies for overseas needs; the Joint Distribution Committee, founded during the First World War by a merger of agencies aiding Jews in Europe, was the largest of these. The work of many Zionist agencies was more in the realm of philanthropy than politics; among these were the Jewish National Fund, the Palestine Foundation Fund, and the women's organization, Hadassah. All this philanthropic activity was conducted by independent organizations formally linked with no religious body.

Indeed, this activity—political, cultural, and philanthropic—was so rich and variegated and vigorous compared with the floundering religious life of the twenties that a number of Jewish thinkers, in particular the philosopher and liberal Horace M. Kallen, proposed that the future Jewish life of this country should be built on all the varieties of Jewish expression that had come into existence and not only on Judaism. Kallen envisaged a community in which Jews would be educated in Jewish history and culture, Jewish political movements would flourish, Jewish art and culture would be encouraged, Jewish philanthropy would take care of special Jewish needs, and religion would be only one of the possible expressions of Jewishness.

All this of course raised the question whether the Jews would be unique in maintaining an extensive variety of activities for a special ethnic group; but this could be answered by pointing to the fact that very similar institutions—schools, factions, publications, philanthropies, etc.—existed among other ethnic groups, suggesting that "cultural pluralism" might be the shape of the future in the United States in general.

The assumption that Jewish life could be maintained without Judaism, or alongside it, was given substance not only by the fact that it was being so maintained but also by the rise of a special institutional form, the Jewish Center. The Jewish Center, which became very popular in the twenties and whose popularity has continued to this day, had a variety of institutional origins. One was the Young Men's and Young Women's Hebrew Associations, which had begun as a kind of educational and social center for German Jewish youth in the middle of the nineteenth century (the first one was established in Baltimore in 1854) but which, toward the end of the century, as the tide of immigration grew, had become concerned with adjusting and Americanizing the immigrant and had become barely distinguishable from settlement houses.

A second point of origin for the Jewish Center was the settlement house itself, established in immigrant communities to teach English and manners to the newcomers and to keep them occupied with hobbies and recreations. Some of these had been specifically Jewish settlement houses, supported by Jewish philanthropists and staffed with Jewish social workers. The first of these was the Educational Alliance, established on the Lower East Side of New York in 1891.

The third important origin of the Jewish Center was the synagogue center movement started in 1918 by Mordecai Kaplan of the Jewish Theological Seminary, when he founded the Jewish Center in New York. Its aim was to make the synagogue more attractive by adding to the house of worship and the school a variety of non-religious activities that might serve the entire surrounding Jewish community. A number of Reform rabbis had pioneered even earlier than Rabbi Kaplan with an "open" or "institutional" temple, for example, Moses Gries, who was rabbi of the Temple in Cleveland from 1892 to 1917.

In the twenties and thirties, the YMHA's had less occasion to act as settlement houses, and the settlement houses themselves found their original functions changing. As the Jewish population in the lower-class neighborhoods moved off to areas of second and third settlement, the Jewish community was faced with the prospect of either abandoning the settlement house or moving it and making it into a middle-class recreational center. In community after community, this transformation was accomplished and a new Jewish Center was established. In many other communities, a center was established from the first, not as a settlement house for the poor, but as a center for a predominantly middle-class population. The YMHA's and YWHA's, too, now began to serve a predominantly middle-class population. And the synagogue centers from the beginning were identified, not with immigrants but with established middle-class communities.

In the twenties and thirties, the center suggested to a number of people that it might be the nucleus for a new type of Jewish community. Its focus would be not religion but something we may call "Jewishness," which would be the common element in a variety of activities—religious, political, cultural, intellectual, philanthropic, all of them legitimately Jewish. This type of community, it was hoped, would replace the dying East European Orthodoxy and maintain Judaism in a new form adapted to America.

While neither Reform nor Orthodoxy could have much to do with such a community of Jews, among whom religion was to be only one of a number of possible expressions of Jewishness, there was one religious movement in American Jewish life that could hope to gain from such a development. This was Conservative Judaism, the growing movement around the Jewish Theological Seminary in New York. We have described how this institution, founded by the old Orthodox Sephardic and Ashkenazic elements in the 1880's, had been reorganized in the early 1900's under a board of wealthy German Reform Jews, with a faculty of East European and German scholars, to train a student body of East European Jewish immigrants and, later, the children of East European immigrants to be modern American rabbis. In 1913, its president, Solomon Schechter, had organized a small group of synagogues into the

United Synagogue of America to create a central body for the congregational tendency between Reform and Orthodoxy represented by the Seminary. The United Synagogue of America grew rapidly during the twenties and thirties. Just as the student body of the Seminary was made up of the children of East European Orthodox parents who found Orthodoxy too severe and Reform too un-Jewish, so also the synagogues that affiliated with the Conservative movement were made up of the more successful East European Jews who wanted to move away from an Orthodoxy barely responsive to a new environment but who also found the services of the Reform synagogue cold and too distant from anything they knew as Jewish. Perhaps, furthermore, they found the members of the Reform synagogue of too high a social and economic level.

But there were more significant elements in the growth of Conservatism, and to understand them we must go back to Solomon Schechter, who had died in 1915. I have pointed out that all aspects of Judaism were attractive to Schechter. He was no ideologue. And this undifferentiated love of Jewishness was to prove the boon of the Conservative movement, because it gave it points of contact with non-religious Jewish life. Thus, Schechter had emphasized the importance of studying Hebrew. This stemmed from his traditional Judaism, his Zionism, and his concern for scholarship. In addition, the Seminary, because of Schechter's influence, because of its faculty, because of its East European student body, was generally friendly to Zionism, even though Cyrus Adler was himself not a Zionist. The Zionist sentiments of the Seminary and its advocacy of Hebrew brought it in touch with some of those secular Jewish elements that played such an important role in Jewish life after the arrival of the East European Jews.

A Teachers' Institute had been founded at the Seminary in 1909, with funds supplied by Jacob Schiff, under the principalship of

Mordecai Kaplan. In 1912, it was decided to conduct the classes of the Teachers' Institute entirely in Hebrew. The Teachers' Institute that was later to be established at Yeshiva College, under Orthodox auspices, and other institutes set up in other cities followed suit, and education in Hebrew, the Hebrew of modern Palestine, became the keystone in the education of teachers for Jewish schools of all types in America. The Jewish teacher that was graduated from this institution was more typically a Zionist than a religious Jew, though of course many were both. This institute attracted many students to the Seminary who did not feel strongly about religion but did feel strongly about the Jewish people and Jewish culture—about Jewishness. In 1919, the Seminary established extension classes in which those who did not want as intensive a Jewish education as that given by the Teachers' Institute might learn Hebrew and study the Bible, Jewish literature, and Jewish history.

With this extensive Conservative program, Reform Judaism, of course, could not compete. Its central religious educational institution, Hebrew Union College, was established in Cincinnati, far from the major centers of Jewish population; moreover, it was somewhat anti-Zionist. As such, it could not hope to be effective in attracting the secular, Zionist element that came to the Seminary's Teachers' Institute and extension classes. Stephen Wise, a major leader of Zionism and a Reform rabbi too, did establish a Jewish Institute of Religion in New York in 1922, hoping to combine the Zionist orientation of the Seminary with the religious freedom of Hebrew Union College. This institution never became as important as either Hebrew Union College or the Jewish Theological Seminary.

The Seminary did not try to justify in any elaborate way the fact that it served as an institution in which many people who had no strong feeling for the Jewish religion were educated. Following the lead of Schechter, it accepted much that was not formally religious as having a place in its program—in particular, the modern Hebrew culture coming out of Zionism. Of course, in this it also followed Jewish tradition, with its refusal to make any sharp distinction between the Jewish religion and the Jewish people. The problem, however, was that events had created such a distinction, and for the first time there were major Jewish movements and institutions that were in no way part of the historical amalgam of people and religion that was Judaism.

The professors of the Seminary, devoted to their scholarly studies, offered little guidance on these problems. Only one professor attempted to deal with the problem created by the existence of this actively Jewish, but non-Judaic, life. More than seeing it as a problem, indeed, Mordecai Kaplan saw it as the opportunity for the revival and strengthening of Judaism in America. Kaplan was the only member of the Seminary faculty who, although born in Europe, had been brought up and educated in the United States (he had gone to City College in New York), and this background was certainly significant in leading him to adopt what we might call a sociological approach to the Jewish religion. I have already spoken of the Jewish Center which he organized in 1918 and of his work as the head of the non-rabbinical teaching of the Seminary. In these activities, he came in touch with the whole range of Jewish life in America and found much material to ponder in his efforts to develop a contemporary approach to Judaism. During the twenties, Kaplan developed his ideas of strengthening Judaism by tying it up with all other aspects of Jewish life, and, in 1934, he published his magnum opus, *Judaism as a Civilization.*

In this book, he argued that Judaism was not a religion, as the West understood this term, but a religious civilization. He described perceptively the breakdown of the organic Jewish community that had unified all Jewish life and argued for the re-establishment of central Jewish communities in America, in which the activities now conducted by a variety of organizations, some religious, would be influenced by a central body representing all Jews. Non-religious Jews were to have a place in this proposed community alongside Reform, Conservative, and Orthodox Jews.

Kaplan's specific proposals for a Jewish community were less important than the tendency of thought he represented, one in which religion, Zionism, and other Jewish interests would combine to form a Jewish civilization. He naturally had to consider the place such a civilization could have in America, and he saw that it created a problem. He found in the existence of Catholicism something of a model for Judaism. "The parochial schooling, the interdict against intermarriage, and the teachings, both direct and indirect, with regard to disbelievers, cannot but have the effect of placing obstacles in the way of free social and economic intercourse between Catholics and non-Catholics, thus countering the trend toward homogeneity which is the goal of democratic nationalism. . . . The rivalry between Catholics and Protestants will keep the United States sufficiently Christian to make Jews realize that by merging with the general population they will not advance one whit the cause of democratic nationalism."[3]

But it was essentially Kaplan's liberalism, both in politics and in religion, that led him to feel that Jewish separateness would not create a serious problem: America after all, whatever the natural tendency of democratic nationalism, did permit separateness of religion, the major component of the religious civilization. Further, Kaplan himself strongly urged the revision of Jewish traditional ideas, such as that of the chosen people, the effect of which might limit or inhibit Jewish harmonization with the rest of the American people. This revision was all the easier for him since, a naturalist and a liberal, he approached religion primarily from the viewpoint of its utility.

In the 1920's, 1930's, and 1940's, Kaplan raised up many disciples at the Jewish Theological Seminary. These were boys from Orthodox homes whose faith had been as little able to survive America as that of most children of Orthodox parents. However, these students were characterized by a strong attachment to Judaism, its customs, its languages, its national hopes, its culture. Kaplan was the salvation of these students. And here his naturalistic theology played an important part; he explained how one could be a Jew (and more, a rabbi) even if, in one's heart, one did not believe in the God of Abraham, Isaac, and Jacob. As Kaplan wrote, "From the standpoint of the Religious-Cultural program [that is, his program], whatever helps to produce creative social interaction among Jews rightly belongs to the category of Jewish religion, because it contributes to the salvation of the Jews."[4] And again: "For the Jew who approaches Judaism as a civilization, the test for any form of adjustment will not be whether it conforms to the accepted teachings of revelation, or whether it is consistent with the universal aims of mankind. His criterion will be: does that adjustment proceed from the essential nature of Judaism? Will it lead to the enrichment of the content of Jewish life? Is it inherently interesting?" These three criteria may be in conflict. Kaplan adds: "It is the feature of interest, rather than that of the supernatural origin or rationality, which is—which must be—the essential factor in the approach to Judaism."[5]

Kaplan abrogated the divine law, just as the Reform rabbis of the nineteenth century had done. But they had abrogated it so that the Jews could be a denomination; Kaplan abrogated it so that the Jews could be a people. They had attacked the supernatural origins of the religious law because they did not want to observe the customs it sanctioned. Kaplan attacked the divine authority of the law because people could no longer honestly believe in it and because a new basis for the observance of Jewish particularity thus became necessary. In the idea of a "religious civilization" Kaplan provided a rationale for Jews who no longer believed in the divine origin of Jewish religious law but nevertheless wanted to keep on living as Jews.

In 1935, Kaplan founded the Reconstructionist movement to propagate his ideas among American Jews in general and in the Conservative movement, where he had his greatest strength, in particular. Kaplan formed the "left wing" of Conservatism, for he was ready to guide himself by contemporary needs rather than by the revealed law. However, despite his theoretical radicalism, he did not in practice go so far in his reforms as some nineteenth-century rabbis who are honored as forerunners of Conservatism; for to him the ceremonies and rituals of Judaism were very important as the cement of the Jewish people.

By the thirties, and even more so the forties, Conservatism was very different from the Conservatism of Adler and Schechter. The East European Jews were no longer the wards of the movement: they were the movement. Louis Finkelstein, son of an East European Orthodox rabbi, succeeded Adler as president of the Jewish Theological Seminary and as leader of the Conservative movement in 1940, and by that year East European Jews dominated the movement completely.

As Conservatism grew, its problems grew. What position should it take on the Jewish law—accepted by the Orthodox, rejected by the Reform group? For Conservatism the main issue was the law as it affected personal observance, for example, the laws of rest on the Sabbath and the dietary laws. In practice, the faculty of the Seminary and the rabbis who graduated from it accepted the law, the laity rejected it. There seemed no way of resolving the dilemma. The smallest adaptation of the ancient law, made by the Conservative rabbis in their annual Rabbinical Assembly, was sure to meet stern resistance from the scholars on the faculty of the Seminary, not to mention violent opposition from the Orthodox. And any effort to revise the law in order to bring it within hailing distance of the practice of the laity seemed hopeless. Every year the rabbis addressed themselves to the dilemma, and every year saw them as far from solution. How could they abandon God's law? And how could they bring a recalcitrant laity to observe it? In Conservatism, which was growing more rapidly than either of the other two tendencies in American Judaism, the dilemma of Judaism as a whole presented itself most sharply.

Rejecting Kaplan's theory, the Conservative movement adopted Kaplan's practice. Conservatism became the movement of those Jewish people who were friendly to all "positive" Jewish tendencies, hoping that out of them would emerge, somehow, an American Judaism.

Meanwhile, what of Reform? In 1940, Reform was still stronger in congregations and in wealth, if not in members, than the growing Conservatism. But Reform too, strangely enough, was being swept back toward the mainstream of Jewish religion and toward an emphasis on the Jewish people, despite the theory of the Reform movement. The explanation of how this came about is to be found in the impact of East European immigration, from which even Reform was not immune. In 1894, Isaac Mayer Wise could say, "[The Central Conference of American Rabbis] includes not the Polish, Russian, and other so-called Orthodox congregations and their teachers, as the Central Conference at once rejected all illiberal elements, and stands only . . . for the American Israel of the liberal and progressive school which, in fact, is the majority of our people."[6] In 1897 the Central Conference unanimously adopted a resolution "that we totally disapprove of any attempt to establish a Jewish state."[7] In those years, too, Reform moved closer and closer to the practice of liberal Christianity with scarcely a dissenting voice.

We do not know how far this development would have gone under unchanged conditions. However, it was reversed by the tide of East European migration. Here we come to an interesting effect of social identification or what we may call simple labeling on social reality. The German Jews were known as Jews; the East European Jews were also known as Jews. Now the differences between them, by almost any set of criteria, were greater than the social differences one would have found in any Protestant denomination in America. Yet the common identification, Jew, led the smaller group, the German Reform Jews, to approximate in some aspects of its behavior the rapidly Americanizing, larger, East European Jewish group. This process could be seen at work in many ways.

For one thing, the simple example of East European Jewish life, while repellent to most German Jews, nevertheless offered a model of a kind of Jewish life that had some influence among them. They could see customs and observances that they had never known and that were attractive to some. This example was given, not only to German Jews with a philanthropic and educational interest in East European Jews, and there were many such, but to German Jewish storekeepers, who had East European Jewish customers; manufacturers hiring East European Jewish labor; and professional men serving East European Jewish clients.

Their common interest, furthermore, led to a drawing together of German Jews and East European Jews. Thus, a German Jewish professional man found in the East European Jews a "natural" clientele. To the East European Jew, Germany and the Germans represented the height of modern science, and the German Jewish doctor could be sure of finding respectful and even worshipful patients among the East Europeans. In addition, he could speak German and so make himself understood to Yiddish-speaking patients. The occasional German Jewish aspirant to office now might find a "natural" voting bloc and would throw into his campaign speeches a few Yiddish words to produce a bond of Jewish fellow feeling. In time, German Jews came to represent large constituencies of East European Jews, and this generally meant that the representative had adopted East European values with regard to Zionism and other questions.

We may see another source of East European influence on German Jewish life in the fact that the great migration added to American Jewish life not only numbers but issues. The ideological ferment in the East European Jewish community over such questions as Zionism, Jewish culture, the Jewish future, assimilation, Yiddish or Hebrew, Jewish education, was transferred from Russia to America, and a new intensity was thus brought into the discussion of these questions in this country. The middle-class uniformity with which Jewish matters were discussed in America was broken, and issues were now argued from unexpected points of view and with unprecedented intensity. This meant that young Jews of the established community in this country who would previously have found nothing in internal Jewish life to interest them could become involved in Jewish matters. For example, American Zionism, had it not been for the great migration, would probably have remained the special interest of a small group instead of becoming a political movement. The East European Jews supplied the mass base, the knowledge, and the intensity which made Zionism in America a large and complex movement with many tendencies, capable of attracting and using the talents of such men as Louis M. Brandeis, Henry Morgenthau, and others from the long-settled Jewish community. Without the East European migration, there is little question that these men, and many others, would have found very little to interest them in American Jewish life.

But beyond all this, I think, were the almost imperceptible influences of the fact that the connotation of "Jew" in the American mind changed. In 1880 it meant, mostly, a German middle-class individual. By 1920 the German element played little part in the identification of the Jews. This change in the meaning of the term "Jew" in the American language led to a certain resistance to and denial of Jewish traits on the part of the German Jews. But it also led to more conformance with historical Judaism by many German Jews.

The story of what happened in Sioux City, Iowa, as told by Martin Hinchin, is revealing. The first Jewish organization in the town, formed by its first German Jewish immigrants, was a Jewish Cemetery Association organized in 1869. Apparently the community was too small to start a temple. But in 1892, a Unitarian church was formed and a number of Jews became active in it, one as a trustee. The Unitarian minister performed marriages for the Jewish group, and it seemed reasonable to expect the Jews, in time, to disappear into the Unitarian church (in other places this may well have happened). However, just about this time East Europeans started to come to Sioux City and immediately, in 1888, formed a Jewish congregation, the first in the city. In 1895, the German Jewish Ladies Aid Society put on a fair to raise money for a temple, at which oysters, a forbidden food, were served, suggesting the degree of assimilation reached. The first Reform services in Sioux City were held in 1898, and in 1901 a Reform temple was built and dedicated. Among its founders were Jews who had formerly been active in the Unitarian church. Does not this sequence of events suggest that it was the example of East European Jewish life that finally led the German Jews to organize a temple? Perhaps one might even say—though of course one can tell nothing of the motivation from the dry account of events—that they were shamed into it. This is of course an extreme example; no other group of Jews seems to have withdrawn from a Unitarian church to form a temple. Yet this story suggests the kind of impact East European Jews had on Reform Judaism.

By 1900 or 1910, as I have said, the rationalistic tendency in Reform Judaism had led to the elimination from the Reform service of almost every aspect of traditional Jewish worship, except for the retention of Hebrew. It was also around this time that Reform had quite definitely lost its *élan*. Between 1900 and 1920, Reform just about held its own. In the twenties there was an influx of more prosperous East European Jewish elements into the Reform temples, and, by 1930, Jews of East European descent already formed half of the Reform membership. Around the same time, in the early twenties, agitation began to introduce more ritual and ceremonial, more "emotion," into the Reform service and to change the *Union Prayer Book*, which had been in use since 1896. In addition, the small group of Zionist rabbis that had been found in the Reform movement from the very beginning grew both in numbers, as more and more rabbis were drawn from the East European group, and in aggressiveness, as a greater and greater proportion of their congregants, also drawn from eastern European immigrants, shared their sympathies.

The pressure within Reform to modify its extreme antinational and antitraditional position became stronger after Hitler's persecution of the German Jews began in 1933. Zionism became an immediate issue as many thousands of German Jews emigrated to Palestine; and the persecution of the Jewish "race" regardless of the religion of individual Jews made it harder to think of the Jews as only a religion.

By the middle thirties, the "classic" Reform position was held by only a minority of the Reform rabbis. In 1935, the Central Conference of American Rabbis, the organization of the Reform rabbis, adopted a position of neutrality on Zionism. Thus was abandoned a position of official hostility first adopted almost forty years before, in 1897. In 1937 the Reform rabbis adopted a new fundamental statement at Columbus, Ohio, which was to supersede the Pittsburgh Platform. Its differences from the Pittsburgh Platform were generally more in tone than in actual assertion, but they were major. For, by 1937, Reform Judaism was the expression of another world, the world of eastern Europe, which, no matter how modified by America, now stamped its character upon the old movement of the German Jews.

The first section of the new statement was closest to the classic Reform position, asserting that the message of Judaism is universal and that "Reform Judaism recognizes the principle of progressive development in religion."

The second, on God, asserted "the doctrine of the One, living God [note: not "God-idea"] who rules the world through law and love." Most striking was section four, boldly headed "Torah" (the traditional Hebrew expression for the body of Jewish law). It asserted that "certain . . . laws have lost their binding force with the passing of the conditions that called them forth," but went on to say, "As a depository of permanent spiritual ideals, the Torah remains the dynamic source of the life of Israel."

And then section five, on Israel, completely repudiated the basis of the Reform position that the Jews are a religion, and a religion alone: "Judaism is the soul of which Israel is the body. Living in all parts of the world, Israel has been held together by the ties of a common history, and above all, by the heritage of the faith. Though we recognize in the group-loyalty of Jews who have become estranged from our religious tradition, a bond that still unites them with us [which is also, it may be noted, Mordecai Kaplan's position], we maintain that it is by its religion and for its religion that the Jewish people has lived. The non-Jew who accepts our faith is welcome as a full member of the Jewish community.

"In all lands where our people live, they assume and seek to share loyally the full duties and responsibilities of citizenship and to create seats of Jewish knowledge and religion. In the rehabilitation of Palestine, the land hallowed by memories and hopes, we behold the promise of renewed life for many of our brethren [note that they are not "coreligionists"]. We affirm the obligation of all Jewry to aid in its upbuilding as a Jewish homeland by endeavoring to make it not only a refuge for the oppressed but also a center of Jewish culture and spiritual life."[8] This is, in effect and detail, a Zionist statement: both a bitter minority and a triumphant majority considered it as such.

In the same year the Union of American Hebrew Congregations, the central body of the Reform congregations, passed a resolution unanimously urging the restoration of traditional symbols and customs, calling for the use in the synagogue of Jewish music sung by Jewish singers and, if possible, by a cantor. It should be recalled that one of the major battles of the early Reformers was for choirs which included, if need be, Gentile singers. In 1940, a revised version of the *Union Prayer Book* appeared. It was substantially the same as the old, but all the changes were in the same direction: away from the extreme position taken by Reform at the beginning of the century. Friday-night service now begins with a candle-lighting ceremony, a traditional home observance of Jews now transferred to the synagogue; and the Kiddush, the prayer over wine for Friday night, is restored. The new revision of the *Union Prayer Book* was unsatisfactory to many rabbis who continued to demand that it be revised further in the direction of the traditional prayer book.

But what was the significance of these developments in Reform Judaism? Did the growing acceptance of Zionism and of traditional Jewish practice indicate a development within Reform toward Judaism, the traditional Jewish religion? Or toward "Jewishness," that concern with Jewish culture, politics, and communal life characteristic of many Jews who had no particular religious beliefs and allegiances? In 1940 it would have been hard to decide between these two interpretations. Undoubtedly both played a role, because of the influx of new East European elements into American Reform; for, within this new group, the conflict between Judaism and Jewishness was still unresolved.

In 1937–38 the synagogue, in all its forms, represented a minority of the American Jews. The *American Jewish Year Book* estimated that Reform congregations in that year had fifty thousand members, Conservative congregations seventy-five thousand members, and Orthodox congregations around two hundred thousand members; all three together could count as members and their families between one and one and a half million Jews, between one-fourth and one-third of all the Jews in the country. The strength of the synagogue was greater among the aged than among the young, and it was not possible to predict any great increase of members.

But, as we know, in the next fifteen years everything changed. Jewishness was everywhere in retreat, and Judaism showed a remarkable, if ambiguous, strength among American Jews.

VII

The Jewish Revival
1945–56

Developments in American Judaism after World War II were accompanied, and in large measure caused, by a new internal migration, this time from the areas of second and third settlement to the suburbs, and from the dense residential districts of the cities to small towns on the outskirts of the major metropolitan centers. This movement of the forties and fifties, like that of the twenties, was itself the effect of major social changes taking place in the Jewish community. These changes raised the East European Jews to the level of wealth and social status already attained by the German Jews around 1880 and have thus wiped out most of the distinctions between the two. Henceforth it was hardly meaningful to speak of East European and German Jews, for, while the distinctions still existed in the awareness of both groups, they were of little effect in any aspect of life. They did not serve to prevent social mixing and intermarriage, nor were there any important organizations entirely or principally German Jewish. The members of the Reform movement and of the American Jewish Committee were after World War II differentiated from those of other organizations more by higher income than by different social origins.

The Jewish Revival

The movement among Jews toward business and the professions and away from occupations of lower income and lower social status, which could be observed even during the depression of the thirties, was greatly accentuated by the economic prosperity accompanying the Second World War and continuing into the postwar years. The result of this movement, as well as the normal effects of age among the immigrants, was to further reduce the Jewish working class to the point where it forms today no significant part of the Jewish population. The Jewish Labor Committee, the major organization representing in the Jewish community what might be considered the point of view of Jewish workers, increasingly represented in the 1950's the Jewish officials of unions largely non-Jewish in membership. It no longer represented a large body of Jewish skilled workers as it did when it was formed in 1934.

As a result, the Jewish community became remarkably homogeneous in its social composition, as homogeneous as the American Jewish community on the eve of the East European immigration. A few figures will illustrate these changes. Between 1948 and 1953, surveys were conducted of the Jewish population in fourteen cities. Some of the largest Jewish communities were included in this group (Los Angeles and Newark), as well as some very small ones (Port Chester and Utica, New York). They offered a fairly good cross-section of American Jews around 1950. The proportion of Jews in non-manual occupations (that is, the professions, business, and white-collar work) ranged from 75 to 96 per cent of all gainfully employed Jews (the higher percentages were to be found in the smaller communities). Within the category of non-manual work, the tendency among Jews was to concentrate in the occupations of higher income and higher status. Thus, comparing this group of communities with another group of ten communities surveyed between 1935 and 1945, the average proportion of professionals had risen from 11 to 15 per cent of the gainfully employed, while the proportion of those engaged as clerks or salesmen had fallen from about 37.5 per cent to 27 per cent. The economic advantage that had been built up in previous years, even during the hard years of the depression, in the form of superior education and experience in business bore fruit in the years of prosperity, and American Jews became an extremely prosperous group, probably as prosperous as some of the oldest and longest-established elements of the population of the United States.

As we have seen, in the period just before the Second World War the issue between "Judaism" and "Jewishness" among American Jews was in doubt. By the end of the Second World War, however, and certainly within a few years after its end, the issue was settled: Jewishness as a program for life in America —that is, the idea that the Jews in America could continue as a group defined not primarily by religion but by secular culture and quasi-national feeling—was recognized as impossible. And Judaism, in all its branches, was flourishing.

Jewish statistics demonstrating this "Jewish revival" are as unreliable as any other privately collected statistics. Nevertheless, even viewed critically, the changes shown by the figures are impressive. Conservatism, which claimed 250 synagogues and 75,000 member families in 1937, claimed over 500 congregations and 200,000 families in 1956. Reform, with 290 temples and 50,000 families in 1937, reported 520 congregations and 255,000 families. The total number of synagogues in the country did not rise much in fifteen years—about 3,700 in 1937 to about 3,900 in 1952. This relatively static number, however, concealed a great change in the type of synagogue included in the figures. In the intervening fifteen years, hundreds of tiny Orthodox congregations in the slum areas of cities had closed; they had been replaced by hundreds of large and vigorous synagogues—Conservative and Reform, as well as Orthodox—on the outskirts. Conservatism and Reform thus grew greatly, partly at the expense of Orthodoxy, for their new adherents were defecting Orthodox Jews and, more significantly, the children of the Orthodox.

But even Orthodoxy, despite the fact that it fed the growth of the Conservative and Reform groups, showed a remarkable vigor. This vigor was expressed in a variety of ways. First of all, its institutions of higher learning were strong and growing. Yeshiva College, founded by the Rabbi Isaac Elchanan Yeshiva in 1928, grew into a university with many divisions, great fund-raising power, and the loyalty of a wide stratum of American Jewry. Orthodox yeshivas educated and graduated larger numbers of scholars than ever before. Conservatism had always drawn on the children of Orthodox parents, and more particularly on the students of Yeshiva College, for its rabbis. Half the rabbinical students of Jewish Theological Seminary in 1955 came from Orthodox homes, and close to a quarter had received their B.A.'s from Yeshiva College. Many more than a quarter of the students had received their preliminary rabbinical education in Orthodox institutions.[1] Indeed, it was for the most part only in Orthodox institutions that it was possible, even in 1956, to acquire the intensive education in rabbinical literature that was considered essential for the Conservative rabbinate.

But more than this, Orthodoxy had shown amazing strength in its elementary and secondary schooling. The all-day schools, often called "yeshivas" for no good reason, in which students spend half their time on Jewish subjects and half on the normal curriculum, grew considerably after 1940. In the middle thirties there were perhaps three thousand children in such schools. Twenty years later there were thirty thousand in them, and the number was continually rising. In 1953, 6 per cent of the Jewish children of New York City attended these schools, twice as many as attended non-Jewish private schools. In the middle thirties the all-day schools had been largely limited to lower-class neighborhoods; by the mid-fifties they had successfully penetrated middle-class neighborhoods. A number of strong central bodies were established to support these schools. While the growth of these schools certainly reflected, in part, the immigration into this country of extremely Orthodox Hasidic groups who were uprooted by Hitler, in larger part they were a native outgrowth of a long-acclimated American Orthodoxy. More than that, there was a strong sentiment among the Conservative laity and rabbis to establish such schools under Conservative auspices, and a few were started. This educational development thus could not be discounted as simply one of the exotic effects of Orthodoxy, soon to disappear.

Therefore, while Orthodoxy still declined in numbers and still found it difficult to establish footholds among the more prosperous and Americanized sections of the Jewish community, it nevertheless showed considerable strength, particularly in the field of education.

Although the direction of change was clear, its dimensions were uncertain. An interesting study of Jewish families in a middle-sized eastern city in 1952 (it had a population of 128,-000, 8,500 of them Jews) suggested what might be the size of these movements among American Jews: 81 per cent of the grandparents of these families had been, or were, Orthodox,

The Jewish Revival

while only 16 per cent of the parents still described themselves as Orthodox. Five per cent of the grandparents had been Reform; 30 per cent of the parents were Reform. Eleven per cent of the grandparents had been Conservative; 43 per cent of the parents now considered themselves Conservative. The adolescent children of these parents were asked, "What do you think you will be when you are married and have your own family?" The investigators reported: "We find that the bulk of young people who come from Reform or Conservative homes expect to remain Reform or Conservative. This is true of 62 per cent of the Conservative and 60 per cent of the Reform homes. Nonconforming Conservative adolescents tend toward Reform Judaism; non-conforming Reform adolescents tend toward Conservatism. . . . Only one out of every five of the children from Orthodox homes intends to remain Orthodox. . . . Most indicate their intentions to become Conservative."[2]

These figures suggest the situation in a single community; but the community was not untypical, and showed what would hold, roughly, for all American Jewry.

Along with the great growth of Conservatism and Reform, and the growing vigor (amid declining numbers) of Orthodoxy, there was a remarkable increase in the number of Jewish children receiving some type of religious education. There were about 230,000 children in Jewish schools (about half in Sunday schools) in 1946, about 400,000 (with the same proportion in Sunday schools) in 1954. It is hardly likely that the Jewish population of school age could have risen by 73 per cent in these eight years. In New York City there was a considerable rise in the proportion of children attending Jewish schools. Whereas in the mid-thirties it was estimated that about 25 per cent of Jewish children of elementary school age attended

Jewish schools in New York City, in 1955 it was estimated that this figure had risen to 31 per cent.

These figures understated the increase in Jewish school enrolment in New York, for many of the families that lived in the city in 1935 had moved to suburban counties by 1955, and in these areas enrolment of children in Jewish schools is higher than in the city. Thus, in 1951/52, when 28 per cent of the children of elementary school age in New York City were enrolled in Jewish schools, 48 per cent of the children of school age in Westchester, Nassau, and Suffolk counties were in Jewish schools. There was a great increase in the numbers attending Jewish high schools in New York City, from 2,500 in 1935 to 7,000 in 1955. And, along with this, there was the development, owing in good measure to the strong interest of the Jewish community, of Hebrew teaching in the public high schools and even junior high schools. In 1954, over 5,000 high-school and junior-high-school pupils in New York City, the overwhelming majority of them Jewish, were taking courses in Hebrew.

As to the quality of this schooling, the signs were contradictory, and the conclusion should probably be that it was neither as good nor as bad as that of earlier years. The growth of large and powerful congregations had sapped the strength of the small and ineffective, private, one-teacher schools and of the large communal schools, those with no synagogical affiliation and serving the entire community, generally with communal funds. While both kinds of schools were Orthodox in tendency, the communal schools were also professional and thorough; the rising synagogues insisted, in community after community, on educating the children of their own members and withdrawing them from the communal schools. This meant a decline in the quality of education for those children who would have attended communal schools, while perhaps those children who would have attended the disappearing, private, one-teacher schools were receiving a better education. On the other hand, the synagogical schools, as they grew, tended to improve. In both the Conservative and the Reform movements, Sunday schools were under continual attack as ineffective, and while the proportion of weekday schools had not increased between 1945 and 1956, the fact that the same proportion had been maintained while the school population had risen greatly was an achievement. The professional standards for teachers were rising (which, together with rising enrolment, created a serious shortage of teachers), and the quantity and quality of textbooks improved.

Even what may be described as personal piety had increased. The demands of traditional Judaism in the sphere of personal religious observances are so great that one could expect only decline from the East European standard. But a certain modified American standard of piety by which one attended services, lit candles on Friday night, and observed the major holidays was on the increase. Again, as in the case of education, Jews were neither as good nor as bad, judged by traditional practices, as they had been; a middle level was taking over.*

This was perhaps first foreshadowed in the Reform group. It had been observed by chaplins in the army that the boys from Reform homes, who knew least about the service (which in the army was standardized close to the Orthodox norm), were

---

* One can find documentation for this point of view in two valuable studies published in the 1960's, *Jewish Identity on the Suburban Frontier: A Study of Group Survival in the Open Society*, "The Lakeville Studies," Vol. I, by Marshall Sklare and Joseph Greenblum (New York, 1967); and *Jewish Americans: Three Generations in a Jewish Community*, by Sidney Goldstein and Calvin Goldscheider (Englewood Cliffs, N.J., 1968).

most dutiful in attendance. In the mid-fifties the same might have been said of most of American Jewry: it knew less, but did more. In 1947, a national public opinion poll had shown that 18 per cent of Jewish respondents attended services once a month (the comparative figures were 65 per cent for Protestant respondents, 85 per cent for Catholic respondents). Eight years later, another national opinion poll asked whether the respondent had attended services during the past week: no less than 31 per cent of the Jewish respondents had. There is no question that Jews in the United States were still less regular in attendance at religious services than Protestants or Catholics. Further, these figures must be used with caution for there are so few Jews caught in any national poll that the possibility of error is very great. But one observed from personal experience very much the same thing. While there was still no danger of overcrowding at Jewish religious services, attendance had increased.

Leaving figures aside, there seemed to be no question that there was much greater interest in religion among Jews in the mid-fifties than there had ever been before. Commercial publishers found it worth their while to publish books on Jewish theology, and the fact that there were such books written by Americans to be published was itself revealing. There was far more discussion of Jewish religion and its problems in periodicals serving American Jews. We must now try to understand these developments, foreshadowed by nothing in the twenties and thirties.

Two explanations were often heard: Hitler and Zionism. These answers explained something but not much. The two greatest events in modern Jewish history, the murder of six million Jews by Hitler and the creation of a Jewish state in

The Jewish Revival

Palestine, had had remarkably slight effects on the inner life of American Jewry up until the mid-fifties.

As a result of the growing catastrophe in Europe in the thirties and early forties, and the parallel crisis in Palestine, hundreds of thousands of Jews who had had little or nothing to do with Jewish life were drawn into Jewish activities. They contributed to the United Jewish Appeal or worked for it, or joined the Zionist organizations or read books on Zionism. But not many people responded to these events by joining the synagogue—its greatest growth was to come after World War II. Vast sums of money were raised for the relief of European Jews and for the establishment of the Jewish state. In 1946 the United Jewish Appeal raised $101,000,000; this sum increased by $16,000,000 in 1947, and by another $31,000,000 in 1948, to reach a peak of $148,000,000. After that the sums collected for relief and Israel declined, but in 1956 $75,000,000 was raised, and in the following year $82,000,000. Huge organizations grew up to raise and manage these funds. However, all this activity was almost exclusively in the hands of secular institutions in which rabbis and religious groups played little part.

Even more significantly, when collections began to fall after 1948, it was in part because of the conflicting demands for money to build local institutions, largely synagogues but also old-age homes, hospitals, Jewish centers, and other institutions. Those who desired to build synagogues were thus in direct conflict with those who wished to send money overseas to help the survivors of Hitler's massacres and the state which was taking in hundreds of thousands of them.

When Israel was established, there was much talk about what this would mean for American Jewry. It was largely an expression of ebullient feelings. What happened after the state was

American Judaism

established was that the major Zionist political organization, the Zionist Organization of America, rapidly declined. The establishment of Israel meant little for American Judaism specifically. Jewish education had been Zionist in orientation; it remained no less and no more Zionist after the establishment of Israel. Judaism in Israel was represented by an embattled Orthodox minority; there was hardly anything that could be considered liberal religion, either Conservative or Reform. American rabbis who went there to find out what they could learn discovered an unchanged Orthodoxy that was almost completely irrelevant to contemporary interests and problems. There were practical effects of Israel on American Judaism: since it had always been a great reservoir of scholarship, it helped replace Poland as a source of Talmudic scholars for the Orthodox and Conservative movements. In addition, Israelis resident in the United States, temporarily or permanently, formed an important part of the teaching force of American Jewish schools. Since the learning of Hebrew was an important part of the curriculum of these schools, Israelis were ready-made for their needs. But the idea that Israel, once it was established, could in any serious way affect Judaism in America, or Judaism in general, appeared in the 1950's largely illusory.

To my mind, there are more persuasive explanations of the religious revival in American Judaism in the postwar period than either Hitler or Zionism. The changes in American Judaism were linked with the great movement away from the areas of second settlement. It is hard to interpret this development in purely Jewish terms. The movement to the suburbs was a general American phenomenon. It reflected not only a rising American prosperity, in which Jews shared, but a change in the social structure of American life, in which occupations

116

historically linked to the lower class and lower-class ways of life tended to be replaced by occupations linked to middle-class ways of life. But aside from the economic and social shift, though certainly allied to it, was the rise of new values in American life, values that may be included under the general heading of "respectability." The behavior that was associated with the lower and the upper classes—irresponsibility, violence, eccentricity—was increasingly frowned upon, and the pattern of middle-class respectability became in the 1950's the pattern that all Americans wished to follow. The facts demonstrating this development were the steady lowering of the marriage age, the decline in the number of single adults, the great increase in church membership and church attendance, the decline of all extremist political movements, whether left or right. Any understanding of what happened to Jews in the United States required taking into account these large movements which had affected all groups.

The Jewish migration out of the areas of second settlement was a migration of just those elements in the past most immune to Jewish religion, the second and third generation of the East European group. The areas of second settlement, we have seen, were the strongholds of Jewish irreligion and of Jewishness. It was in these almost totally Jewish areas, paradoxically, that Jews could live lives almost completely unaffected by Jewish religion and that the proportion of synagogue members was always lowest. It was in these areas, too, that any special movement in Jewish life, one, let us say, combining attachment to Yiddish, rejection of Zionism, socialism, and insistence on the need for territorial concentration in some area not Palestine, could be reasonably sure of finding a few adherents; for Jews were so numerous there that some of any outlook could be found. And it was in these areas, too, that one could live a completely Jewish life from a sociological point of view and yet have no connection with any Jewish institution, religious or non-religious. It was here, in other words, that one could have only Jewish friends, eat Jewish foods, follow Jewish mores and culture patterns, and yet have little consciousness of being a Jew. But, as these neighborhoods broke up under the impact of prosperity and as new settlements of much lower density were created on the outskirts of the metropolitan centers, a number of social influences began to be felt which simultaneously strengthened Judaism and weakened Jewishness.

Let us consider the situation of a typical Jewish family that migrated from an area of second settlement to a new suburban development. We assume such a family consisted of relatively young parents who had been born in this country and one or two children of pre-school age, or very early school age. This family was now conscious of Christian neighbors, and of what they thought, in a way that was not necessary before. The few non-Jews in the areas of dense Jewish settlement, as the sociologist Marshall Sklare has pointed out, were generally of a social status lower than the Jews, such as janitors or domestic servants who were Catholics or Negroes. They were not "neighbors." The new suburban areas may have been in large measure Jewish, but this generally meant that they contained 25 or 50 per cent Jews, rather than 75 to 90 per cent Jews, as did the areas of second settlement. The neighbors were now of the same or higher social status and very likely Protestant rather than Roman Catholic. In this situation the religious behavior of the Christian neighbor began to impinge on the consciousness and conduct of the Jewish suburbanite. The children went to school with Christian children and played with Christian children, and, when Sunday came, it was embarrassing to have the children playing outside while the Christian children went to Sunday school and church. In moving from the city to the suburbs, the second generation had to become self-conscious about religion.

Further, because the children now played with non-Jewish children on a level of middle-class respectability which did not countenance the name-calling and fist-fighting of the slum and the area of second settlement, it became necessary to supply them with answers. Such questions as "Why am I a Jew?" inevitably arose, and it was harder to answer them in the middle-class suburb where everyone looked alike than in the urban neighborhood where the ethnic groups were marked by outer characteristics, as so many distinct species. The parents knew no answers to these questions, either because they had had no Jewish education or because their Jewish education consisted of a certain degree of traditional observance and some Hebrew and Bible (perhaps even a great deal), which did not serve to answer questions. A new form of Jewish education thus became necessary, and the modern Sunday school and weekday school, designed to adjust children, to teach them why they were Jews, was gratefully accepted. It took over from the parents a task they were incapable of handling.

The problems of the children in the new suburbs were thus a major factor in leading the parents to decide they needed a school. Here, perhaps, was the chance for the advocates of a Jewishness without Judaism to strengthen their position. If the problem faced by the Jewish parent in the suburbs was simply one of getting the children to attend some kind of school on Sunday morning and having them learn some answer to what it meant to be a Jew, there was no reason why this school had to be a religious school, teaching religious doctrine. It could be a secular Jewish school. Certainly, many parents must have considered this possibility, and here and there a school of one of the declining Yiddish school movements had been established in the suburbs. In one case (Park Forest, Illinois), a Jewish school which explained what it was to be a Jew but did not press religious (or Zionist) points of view on the children was attempted. There must have been similar cases of schools which were Jewish, but not Judaist.

However, there were a number of reasons why this combination, even if not impossible, did not generally emerge. The first was simply the institutional vigor of Jewish religious institutions. Central bodies for each of the major Jewish denominational groups—Reform, Conservative, Orthodox—already existed, with their educational departments, their prepared curriculums, their traveling field advisers, their lists of qualified teachers. There were, indeed, non-denominational bureaus for Jewish education in the major cities, but these, with the decline of the communal schools, which had been their major concern, had to be careful not to antagonize their new clients, the denominational, i.e., synagogical, schools. It was much easier for a group of parents to resort to an existing body, with considerable resources, for help in starting a school than to try to start one themselves or to rely on the help of the much smaller groups that still maintain non-religious Jewish schools.

But then, too, in each of these communities there tended to be a core of Jewish families that formerly belonged to synagogues and that wanted to start one in any case. Those who were faced with the problem of the Jewish education of their children and who did not wish it to be religious were confronted with, on the one hand, an existing or beginning congregation that supported an established school and, on the other hand, only their own relatively weak and institutionally unsupported feeling in favor of secular Jewish education. In such a conflict, there was no question which would win out. And even if parents began only by sending their children to the religious school, very soon they themselves would be drawn in, if only by the institutional devices for doing this. The children of non-members could be barred from the synagogue's school—it could truly be asserted it was overcrowded; what school was not?—or the tuition for non-members' children could be made almost equal to the regular family-membership dues which included children's education. Thus, for the sake of the children, many adults became members of synagogues.

But, aside from the institutional strength of the religious Jewish organizations, we must point to the decline of the intellectual basis for Jewishness. It was mostly movements of a socialist orientation that argued for Jewishness; it was an ethnocentric America that had made cultural pluralism a reasonable program. Socialism had been in steady decline since the early thirties, and, when Abraham Cahan's *Forward* came out for Roosevelt in 1936, it symbolized the fact that socialism among the Jews had become simple liberalism. As for cultural pluralism, when mass immigration ended in 1924, every passing year showed that this was no reasonable prospect for America.

We began with the children in trying to explain how it was that Judaism developed with such unexpected vigor among the second- and third-generation Jews in this country. The children were not the whole story, but they were indeed a very important part of it; the Jewish culture of the new suburban areas after World War II was child-centered. The problems of how to raise the children, how to educate them, where to live so that they would have suitable playmates, and so on, made up a good part of middle-class conversation. And among the Jews these concerns were undoubtedly more widespread, because the Jews were more family-centered than perhaps any other large group in the country. A higher proportion married, a lower proportion got divorced, and, in general, fewer adult Jews lived outside of families than was the case among other Americans. Judaism was in large measure being re-created for the children, who played a surprisingly large role in the service of the suburban synagogue and for whom religious festivals were recast so as to emphasize the pleasant and attractive elements.

This description, I fear, will be summed up conveniently but inaccurately in the terms "conformity" or "other-direction." Certainly large elements of both were involved. We can indeed explain the Jewish revival in "sociological" terms as we are doing here, but the fact that we concentrate on them now, for analytical convenience, does not mean that there were no directly "religious" factors which we may conceive of as expressed in some kind of internal demand independent of one's social surroundings and which would lead one to act even against what the social environment expects and encourages. The revival of Judaism, as seen in the increased concern for Jewish education for one's children, had such aspects, too; but we have reserved these for discussion in the next chapter.

The children, then, played a great role, but that is not the whole story, and we must now consider the adults independently of the children. In the Jewish areas of the cities, as we have said, one was a Jew without thinking about it and even without doing anything about it. In the new suburban communities to which hundreds of thousands of Jews moved, it was discovered that, subtly but certainly, American social life, at least in the respectable middle-class suburbs, moved to a large extent within denominational lines. Non-Jews expected that the Jew would have his own social community marked off from Catholic and Protestant communities. Now this enforced social community had the effect of making the secular Jew a "captive audience" for the religious or at least institutional Jew.

In the Jewish city areas, the Jew could select his social milieu, and many of these groups could be expected to consist of persons with no religious or institutional affiliation. In the smaller cities Jews have always been a captive audience for each other because of the small size of the Jewish community. And in such situations, every Jewish institution wins. In Nashville, for example, with less than three thousand Jews and three synagogues, one-half of the families were members of more than one synagogue (many, of all three). Even people who are not particularly attached to the Orthodox synagogue will pay dues out of deference to a parent's wishes. There are so few Jews that most of them know each other and any individual finds it hard to resist the pressure, from those few involved, to help (or save) a Jewish institution. Of course, the existence of a captive audience, that is, a relatively small Jewish community in which each Jew lives his life among other Jews, is only part of the story. There must be some bond of feeling among all Jews before some of them can arouse the guilt-feelings of others and so gain their support for some Jewish institution. Unless this bond of feeling exists, the principle of the captive audience will not operate; for then many Jews, not considering themselves bound to the group, could easily refuse to give their support and easily tolerate the disapproval of their fellows. So, once again, we must warn against any simple interpretation in terms of conformity. There would be no conformity if there did not exist this bond that makes most Jews feel part of the same group.

With migration to the suburbs, then, the situation of the Jews in the smaller communities was reproduced and Jews became a captive audience for the most energetic and aggressive among them. But now, who were the most energetic and aggressive? They were the Judaists, the upholders of Jewish religion, or at least religious institutions. In the postwar era those strongly antireligious Jews who had been socialists or socialist Zionists or Yiddish culturists before the war lost heart for the fight. All these were causes that had clearly had their day. Their simple rationalism was no longer satisfying. We do not wish to discuss the reason for what, in the early forties, was called by the embattled naturalists, "the new failure of nerve"—the flight of intellectuals from rationalism, science, and socialism, and the drift toward religion. Certainly among the Jewish intellectuals the European catastrophe had something to do with it. In the mid-forties, there was a fascinating and moving development among leading Yiddish writers who had been the apostles of rationalism to the Jewish masses for generations. These men, many of them middle-aged and older, returned to religion. It was not rational Reform to which they turned, nor did they undergo dramatic conversions. Overwhelmed by the Jewish catastrophe and the pointlessness of all rational explanations of it, they once again picked up the old burden of the Jewish law, or part of it, started going to the synagogue again, and once again became "observant" Jews. One should not exaggerate the significance of this movement. Indeed, to a sociologist it is invisible, for the few Jewish scholars and journalists who returned to the traditional religion formed no bulge in any conceivable statistics. Still, nothing quite like this had happened in Jewish

The Jewish Revival

life since the Enlightenment first began to influence Jews in the late eighteenth century.

In addition to these ideological developments, there was the general change in the climate of opinion. Most forms of secular Jewishness, I have pointed out, have had some kind of socialist orientation. They suffered with the general decline of socialism in America. These movements had been anticlerical and sometimes even atheistic. They suffered with the general decline of atheism in America and the growing acceptance of religion as a normal part of Americanism. And then, too, the Jewish community, which had once been largely working class, was now almost entirely middle class. How could such a community maintain its attachment to these rather exotic and quite foreign socialist, secular Jewish movements? And if these forms of being a Jew were no longer possible, what was left but religion? If, that is, one wanted to be a Jew.

So, in our collections of captive audiences in the new Jewish communities burgeoning after the war, the naturalists and rationalists and anticlericalists tended to be silent, or at least far more restrained than they would have been fifteen years ago; and the adherents of religious Jewish institutions tended to be aggressive.*

Finally, the religious institutions themselves responded to the needs of these "returning Jews." In the synagogue buildings erected since the war, schoolrooms and community facilities were often more prominent than the synagogue itself. The schoolrooms were not, as in the case of the city synagogue, in

* Of course, Jews outside the suburbs, too, were influenced by their children's needs, their Christian neighbors, and the changing climate of thought and opinion, and the "Jewish revival" was not limited to suburban communities. However, it was seen in its most striking forms there.

basements under the main synagogue. They were in fine, modern buildings designed by leading architects. Similarly, there were now facilities of all kinds from nursery schools to clubrooms for teen-age groups, from meeting places for young married couples to card tables for the old people. Following the advice of Mordecai Kaplan, consciously or unconsciously, the synagogues became "synagogue centers." The religious services often seemed the least vital of the many "services" supplied by the new synagogues. The children almost certainly went to the school, the teen-agers very likely went to the dances, the women probably joined the sisterhood, the men possibly joined the brotherhood, and last—and the rabbi often asked himself if it was also least—were the religious services, poorly attended by a core of old-timers and the merest scattering of young people.

In effect, Mordecai Kaplan's view of the future of Judaism had triumphed—not that he himself was necessarily happy about the result. It was the social needs of the individual Jew, and the communal needs of the entire community, that the synagogue met, and as an institution it was flourishing. During the forties and fifties, people often asked whether the synagogue was meeting the religious needs of Jews. But the Jews themselves did not demonstrate any strong religious drive. They thronged the Jewish centers and the center-synagogues but did not participate in any large numbers in the services of the synagogue. The more sensitive rabbis, regardless of what the statistics showed, still found themselves among a people remarkably resistant to religious feeling. Even the rabbinate was not very different in this respect from the people. One Reform rabbi wrote, in an article entitled "The Rabbi's Personal Religion," "I know of only one Conference [Central Conference of American Rabbis] attempt to consider the religion of the rabbi, and even then it was to determine how the religion of the pulpit reacted upon the people."[3]

The rabbi may have wondered just what his function was. The Jewish law was (except in Orthodox congregations) generally neglected, and the rabbi was no longer called upon to act as judge and interpreter. He could keep himself busy running his expanded synagogue and school and going to interfaith meetings, but did he have any role as a religious guide? In his article "The Rabbi in the Small Town," one rabbi reported: "[The congregants] invariably imply and often explicitly state, 'We need you as our representative among the non-Jews, to mingle with them, to speak in their churches, to make a good impression. We do not need you for ourselves. Well, for the old people, perhaps, and for the children, yes, once a week, but for the Gentiles most of all!' "[4] And one might hear the same comments in larger cities.

To be sure, such an attitude represented an extreme position. More common was the feeling among large numbers of Jews that the institutions of Jewish religion were useful because they contributed to the continued existence of the Jewish people. The ancient notion that Israel existed to serve the law was here reversed: it was argued that the law existed to serve Israel.

This function for institutional religion was directly proposed by one writer and certainly felt, less directly, by many people. C. B. Sherman, himself a Jewish nationalist, pointed out that, in America, peoples—ethnic groups—do not survive as such and that, given the constitution of American society, there was no reason why they should. The theory of cultural pluralism, which assumed there would be some kind of minority rights, was obviously dead. What, then, of those who wanted to see the Jewish people survive? The answer, Sherman said, was that they might survive in the form of a religion. For America did recognize religions.[5]

The same thesis was developed at greater length by Will Herberg in his book *Protestant, Catholic, Jew: An Essay in Religious Sociology* in 1955, and used to explain not only the Jewish religious revival but the postwar strength of Protestantism and Catholicism as well: in each case the desire to maintain community, which had been expressed in ethnic forms, was now being expressed in religious forms.

Was this the whole story? Did the synagogue survive because it satisfied the social and communal needs of Jews and because it enabled the Jewish people to continue in a quasi-religious form appropriate to the American milieu? Or did it satisfy real religious needs? Or is it that the survival of the Jewish people is itself a "religious" need? These are the most difficult questions of all, but any discussion of Judaism in America must come to them.

VIII

The Religion of American Jews

It is a relatively simple matter to record the history of religious institutions and religious thought. But it is generally felt that what is most important about religion is not its institutions or even necessarily the points of view developed by leading thinkers but its place in the lives of ordinary people. We can collect statistics on how many children attend religious schools, how many adults join synagogues; we can describe how schools and synagogues are conducted, what is taught, and what is preached. But what really goes on in the minds of people? Do they attend synagogues because they live in a social milieu in which such behavior seems to them proper? Or are they moved by some desire to relate themselves to a larger community? Or do they wish to make contact with some ultimate reality that some of them call God? How do we decide such questions—after all, the most important for anyone who wishes to understand what is happening to a religion?

We will not get far, I believe, if we attempt to answer such questions by collecting evidence from sociological and social-psychological studies. For the meaning of the evidence we collect is rarely clear. The Gallup Poll, for example, reports that 96 per cent of the American people believe in God.[1] In the face of this evidence, it would nevertheless be possible—and it would require no especially subtle theologian to do so—to argue that simple assertion is no proof and to say that the behavior of the American people demonstrates that they do not—in such an overwhelming proportion, at any rate—"believe in God." Nor, were we to find a very large number of atheists in such a poll, would it require any great sophistication to argue that the atheists, or some of them, really do believe in God, though they say they do not.

Such a simple fact then tells us very little about the religious life of the American people. We could press our social-psychological investigations, make our interviews more intensive, and ask people what they mean when they say they "believe in God." The answers would be more revealing, but would they really enable us to make any direct judgment on the religious life of the American people? Most people are not theologians, most people do not think about what they mean; and I suspect this second stage of an investigation into the religious life of the American people would leave us with a confused mass of data reflecting the various influences of the Catholic catechism, fundamentalist Protestantism, liberal religion, and the agnosticism of earlier years. This would permit us to make a contribution to the social psychology of religion, but we would still be at a loss to understand the extent and nature of authentic belief and feeling in the American people.

At this point we would be forced to proceed to another level altogether. We would go beyond what people say, and even their explanations of what they say, and would try to understand them— from what they say and how they behave. We might conclude with a statement of what the American people believe that they themselves would not recognize, that they might conceivably attack as false and slanderous, but that might nevertheless be true. Belief is not a simple thing; what people think they believe may not be what they really believe, what actually governs their actions. The apparent paradox of this statement can be resolved when we realize that by belief we mean something serious, something that has an impact on life; and what people think they believe may be so superficial and so at variance with their behavior that we may simply have to conclude there are other, more "real" beliefs that we must try to understand.

This reasoning determines the form of the following discussion, in which many things will be said that may hurt Jews and that may seem to have little basis in reality. I can point to no decisive evidence for most of my assertions—I can only refer to all those bits of behavior that suggest to me the real structure of American Jewish religious belief.

Such a procedure is in any case inevitable. Were we to limit ourselves to what American Jews say about their religion, or to what they carry on the surface of their minds, how confused and banal a picture we would carry away! We would find, on the one hand, the clichés of liberal religion and, on the other, a kind of confusion in which loyalty to the Jewish people is identified with Jewish religion. The two are of course related; but there are also distinctions—even for Judaism—between group feeling and religion. If we were to ask American Jews about their religious beliefs, we would find prominent the feeling that religion should keep in step with science, psychotherapy, and liberal politics, and that as long as it does so it is doing its job; the notion that religion is important for Jewish self-respect—a kind of adjunct to the defense agencies engaged in fighting anti-Semitism; the idea that Judaism is important in keeping the Jewish people alive and together—a kind of adjunct to the work of the Zionist groups; and of course many people would hold all these ideas.*

* The work of Marshall Sklare and Joseph Greenblum (referred to in the footnote to page 113) permits one to specify more fully the beliefs of American Jews, but it is consistent with the picture drawn here.

American Judaism

This would be the result of an extensive, well-conducted survey of the religion of American Jews. We would find only a small minority who, asked about the nature of their religious beliefs, would respond with a declaration of faith in the authority of the law, the providence of God, Israel's election, and the coming of the Messiah. Few Jews would know what the principles of the Jewish faith are. Many indeed would justify their confusion by denying that there are any principles. True, the principles have never been pronounced by a single authority acceptable to all; but many great Jewish thinkers have propounded the principles of the Jewish faith, and Maimonides' summary of that faith in thirteen points is included in the traditional prayer book.

American Jews, if they believe in anything, believe in the instrumental efficacy of religion, as do, of course, most American Catholics and Protestants. Judaism is good for the Jew. It keeps him mentally healthy and adjusted, and it keeps the Jewish people together. The conceptions that it is good in itself and that it embodies valuable and unique truths are foreign to the great majority of Jews in this country.

What, one may ask, is the significance of the fact that most American Jews are incapable of giving a coherent statement of the main beliefs of the Jewish religion and tend to call "Judaism" whatever views they happen to hold today? After all, formal theological beliefs have never been greatly emphasized in Judaism; even in its great ages such beliefs have been quite unimportant for the ordinary Jew. For him the issue was not creed and conviction; piety and faith were expressed in acts, in the performance of hundreds of commandments. There are observers of the Jewish religious scene in America today who feel that, in the light of this characteristic of the Jewish religion, it would be an unfortunate sign of Christian influence if Jews were now to start insisting on tenets and doctrine.

Indeed, if the absence of tenets and doctrines were accompanied

132

The Religion of American Jews

by the observance of even the major commandments of the Jewish religion, there would be much virtue in such a position. However, traditional Jewish piety as expressed in the observance of ritual is now to be found among only a small minority of American Jews. Some form of observance, it is true, will be found in almost every Jewish home. One may discover from a study of lay members of Reform synagogues in 1953 that 74 per cent conduct Seders on Passover and 81 per cent light candles on Hanukkah (largely, one may assume, to counter the effects of Christmas: 21 per cent also report they have Christmas trees!). One is surprised to discover that the dietary laws—which are not in any way a requirement of Reform Judaism—are observed by 8 per cent of Reform Jews, and as many as one-quarter will not eat pork. Thus, the remnants of traditional observance are found almost everywhere. Yet it is also true that a Conservative rabbi will take it for granted that he cannot eat in the homes of most of his congregants. A survey of lay leaders of Conservative congregations reports that among these laymen only 37 per cent have kosher homes.*

But more significant than the figures of those adhering to one or another rite is the fact that the pattern of life envisaged by traditional Judaism, which in fact was the way of life of almost all Jews down to the nineteenth century, is now the way of life of only a very small minority of American Jews. There is much in the Jewish religion that is not law and observance. Yet its essence, as developed over a period of two thousand years, was a complete pattern of life, in which a daily round of prayers and observances, punctuated by the more intense observances of the Sabbath and the festivals, reminded all Jews that they were a holy people. This pattern of life was Judaism; today it is maintained by a small minority, and, since

* The studies by Sklare and Greenblum, and Goldstein and Goldscheider, referred to in the footnote on page 113, give further details on Jewish religious observances.

133

only a minority observe it, it has changed its character. The observances are no longer the outward form of the Jew but the ideological platform of only one of several trends in Jewish life. Judaism, which was the religion of all the Jewish people, has become Orthodoxy, which is the position of only some of them. This creates a more serious break in the continuity of Jewish history than the murder of six million Jews. Jewish history has known, and Judaism has been prepared for, massacre; Jewish history has not known, nor is Judaism prepared for, the abandonment of the law.

As we have said, the abandonment of a pattern of religious life made up of the observance of hundreds of commandments has not been replaced by an emphasis on a few central principles or tenets of faith. Nor do we find that the expression of piety and faith by way of the observance of the commandments has been replaced by more direct expressions of religious faith. One might have expected that the acculturation of Jews to American ways in so many spheres of life and thought would be accompanied by a degree of religious acculturation and that the personal religious experience which is so striking a part of American religious life would begin to appear in Jewish life too.

Certainly the contemporary American scene shows nothing of the sort. Indeed, any strong religious feeling is looked upon with suspicion in the Jewish community and often considered a harbinger of conversion to Christianity. But there is generally little occasion for such suspicion to arise. I think there is nothing in American Jewish literature as yet (it is of course still young and not very extensive) that might possibly find a place in any anthology of religious experience. Were William James writing his *Varieties of Religious Experience* today, he would have to supplement his examples with many new personal accounts, but none of them I think would be Jewish—except perhaps for a few Jews who have been converted to Christianity. (In general, the number of actual conversions is extremely small, though probably a sizable number of Jews "pass" and even join churches without actually converting.) In the biographies of American Jews, and of American rabbis too, one will find passions engaged by the problems of Zionism, the conflict of different organizations within Jewish life, by politics and reform movements; but the category of spiritual experience—and, despite what certain rationally minded Jews say, it is a Jewish category as much as a Christian one—is absent.

Cannot one say that all religion has been radically shaken in the modern world and that Judaism is involved in this crisis? This is true, as far as it goes, but it seems to me that Judaism is even more vulnerable to the unsettling influence of modernity than is Christianity. Judaism emphasizes acts, rituals, habits, a way of life. Christianity, in contrast, places more emphasis on beliefs and doctrines. Judaism in its popular form, in the version in which it was taught to the East European Jews who were the fathers and grandfathers of the great majority of American Jews, tended to obscure distinctions between greater and lesser observances, to ignore doctrine even more than medieval Judaism did, and to obscure the meaning of ritual. In effect, it taught a rigid set of rituals to cover one's entire life. This rigidity permitted no defense in depth, so to speak. As I have said, once one had found—as so many immigrants did—that it was more convenient to work on Saturdays or to shave or to abandon traditional dress, one had no body of doctrine to fall back upon that could explain what remained *really* important in Judaism—indeed, the question was whether *anything* was really more important than the rituals established by God's word. Under these circumstances, an entire way of life disintegrated. And thus contemporary Jews, who feel reasonably enough that beliefs should form part of a religion, are more often dependent for an understanding of their own faith on the public relations agencies of Jewish life—which explain that Judaism believes in democracy, the brotherhood of man, and so on—than on their own knowledge.

Christianity is more fortunate. Since its emphasis is so strongly on beliefs, one can abandon some of them and concentrate one's polemical and dialectical resources on the defense of a few fundamental points. On what can Judaism concentrate? One of the major concerns of the Orthodox group in its defense of traditional Jewish religion is the minimum height of the barrier between men and women in the synagogue—a detail exactly in line with the matters discussed by the Jewish sages in the Talmud. How to make such a religion viable in the modern world is indeed a problem.

The disintegration of religion, it is widely believed, has left certain residues, some of them valuable. Thus it is often argued that, while people may no longer believe that each man has a soul, it is nevertheless because they once believed so that they treat other human beings as if they had souls. What residues does the disintegration of the Jewish faith leave behind? What impact remains from that traditional Jewish education that, directly or indirectly, has influenced so many American Jews?

One element of the Jewish tradition, it is often argued, remains alive, even if in secularized form, and still guides Jewish behavior. This is the Jewish concern for social justice. It is not easy to demonstrate that a group is committed to social justice, nor is it easy to know, in many situations, what social justice is; yet I think it is true that American Jews are almost universally to be found among the defenders of civil liberties and civil rights and in favor of policies which improve the position of the workingman. Every public opinion poll shows them holding what we may legitimately call enlightened views. They are generally against the segregation of

Negroes and for the widest possible extension of rights of free speech and free publication; they favor labor unions and support organizations devoted to civil rights and civil liberties; and they read and support liberal publications. Within their own community, they raise large sums of money for the poor and unfortunate, and they contribute to community chests which raise money for non-Jewish agencies. They are concerned with medicine, the development of social work, and psychotherapy. In short, Jews play a significant role, far greater than their numbers suggest, in all the tendencies that come under the heading of liberalism, progress, and reform. Do we not have here a secularized version of the passion for social justice expressed by the Hebrew prophets? Many Jews—and non-Jews—believe so, but the matter is not so simple.

It is hard to see direct links with Jewish tradition in these attitudes; it is rather easier to trace them to the political positions which the Jews, as an underprivileged element in both Germany and Russia, adopted in order to achieve their own political and social liberation. The German Jewish immigrants of the mid-nineteenth century were naturally, for the most part, liberals; for it was the liberal program that promised to strike off the last shackles of medieval restraint. In Russia, the Jews were in such distress that the liberal program did not promise them much. There they took up radical political positions. It is possible they were attracted to socialism in part because of certain elements in the Jewish religious tradition; perhaps more Jewish workers became radicals because their intellectual training, limited as it was, made them aware of the possibility of change and because the messianic elements in the Jewish religion—muted as they were in East European religious education—made it easier for them than for former peasants to envisage the possibility of a radical improvement in their conditions.

But this connection is a highly speculative one. One thing is sure: it is an enormous oversimplification to say Jews in eastern Europe became socialists and anarchists because the Hebrew prophets had denounced injustice twenty-five hundred years before.

When immigrant Jews came to this country, they brought with them, as most immigrants do, the political attitudes they had adopted in Europe. German Jews were liberal and republican in outlook, though, as far as one can tell, they were not intensely concerned with American politics. The secularized East European Jews were largely socialist; the religious Jews, like other urban immigrants, followed the urban political machines, largely Democratic but sometimes Republican. In time, the fervor of Jewish socialists weakened, and in the mid-thirties most of them began to support Democratic candidates—generally by way of the American Labor and Liberal parties. Today, the great majority of American Jews support Democratic candidates, but their allegiance is more to liberalism as such than to the party.

Does the Jewish tradition play a role in this political history? Very likely, but in extremely indirect ways; and I feel it is specious to say that American Jews express religious attitudes indirectly in their concern for social problems. Whatever the *origins* of this concern, it is now divorced from religion. Its strength in the Jewish group has almost always come from non-religious elements.

Indeed, it is one of the most remarkable things about American Judaism, as distinct from American Jews, that it is not particularly concerned with social problems. This is understandable in the case of the Orthodox elements, who have been engrossed with the problems of defending the faith. On the other hand, the failure of a Jewish "social gospel" movement to develop among Reform Jews is really surprising. The "social gospel" was a movement among Protestant ministers in the early twentieth century to make the

Christian religion a force for social justice. We have described how the Reform leaders, in their search for a relevant modern ethical content for Judaism, emphasized the concern of some prophets for social justice. The eighth point in the Pittsburgh Platform of 1885, it will be recalled, declared, "We deem it our duty to participate in the great task of modern times, to solve on the basis of justice and righteousness the problems presented by the contrasts and evils of the present organization of society." But it was not until 1918 that the Central Conference of American Rabbis adopted a statement on social justice.

During the twenties, a Reform Jewish "social gospel" tendency flowered for a while. In 1923, the Central Conference of American Rabbis co-operated with the Federal Council of the Churches of Christ and the National Catholic Welfare Conference in issuing a statement attacking the seven-day week–twelve-hour day in the steel industry, which, together with other expressions of an outraged public opinion, led the steel industry to abandon those barbarous working conditions. The three groups investigated the Western Maryland railroad strike in 1927 and the North Carolina textile strikes in 1929. But with the coming of the depression and the growing strength of the trade-union movement, the importance of the intervention of the churches in industrial disputes declined; and the most promising field that had been opened for the social gospel was closed. No statements on war and peace could possibly have the effect of the united intervention of the churches in an industrial dispute.

The Conservative rabbinical group (the Rabbinical Assembly of America) did not enter the field until 1932, when a committee on social justice issued a report. This statement reflects the Conservative rabbis' awareness of Jewish backwardness: "It does not redound to the credit of the Synagogue and the Rabbinate . . . that the

Church, a religious system alleged to be noteworthy for 'other-worldliness,' should have been the first to speak on questions of social justice . . . while the spokesmen of Judaism, . . . noted for its worldliness and practical idealism, should have been silent. And it is moreover strange that when the synagogue did begin to speak, it was the Reform group which spoke."² In 1934 this Rabbinical Assembly adopted a radical pronouncement on social justice, but it was not much more radical than the statements then being made by some Protestant groups.

For the past forty years, in both the Reform and the Conservative groups, there has been a history of social action and social justice committees and commissions being organized, issuing statements, and becoming dormant, to be reorganized again a few years later. There are frequent complaints about the futility of issuing statements, followed by the issuing of new statements. It is clear that in this area the Reform and Conservative rabbis follow, rather than lead, the Jewish community—and this is not the case in some Protestant denominations where the ministers, even if not leaders on social attitudes, generally express social attitudes in advance of their parishioners.

One explanation, certainly, of the failure of a Jewish "social gospel" to develop is that Jews have been overwhelmed by their own problems since 1933. They have had to rescue hundreds of thousands of Jews from Germany and Austria, help the Jewish community of Palestine, try to save the millions of eastern Europe, aid the new state of Israel, help the endangered Jews of the Moslem countries. It is understandable that rabbis have had little time to worry about the non-Jewish world. Conceivably the strong concern of the Reform Jewish group with general social problems in the 1920's might have been maintained and strengthened in the thirties and forties had it not been for the rise of pressing Jewish problems.

The Religion of American Jews

We have digressed to describe the history of social action in the rabbinical groups in order to make one large point: in Jewish life, it is not the religious element—the rabbis and religious laymen—that makes opinion on social problems. I believe that Jewish social attitudes derive more from nineteenth-century liberalism and socialism than from the Hebrew prophets. The Jewish religious tradition probably does dispose Jews, in some subtle ways, toward liberalism and radicalism, but it is not easy to see in present-day Jewish social attitudes the heritage of the Jewish religion.

What else is there? What in the feelings and sentiments of Jews can we see as reflecting their ancestral religion?

We must begin with something that has not happened; this negative something is the strongest and, potentially, most significant religious reality among American Jews: it is that the Jews have not stopped being Jews. I do not now speak of the fact that they are sociologically defined as Jews; this is of small significance from the point of view of Jewish religion. I speak rather of the fact that they still *choose* to be Jews, that they do not cast off the yoke or burden of the Jewish heritage. Despite the concreteness of the words "yoke" and "burden," what I have in mind is something very abstract. It is not that most Jews in this country submit themselves to the Jewish law; they do not. Nor can they tell you what the Jewish heritage is. But they do know it may demand something of them, and to that demand, insofar as it is brought to them and has any meaning for them, they will not answer No. The significance of the fact that they have not cast off the yoke is that they are prepared to be Jews, though not to be the Jews their grandfathers were. The medieval world is gone and Orthodox Judaism is only a survival (as the anthropologists use the word) so far as the majority of American Jews is concerned. But they are prepared to be some kind of Jews;

they are capable of being moved and reached and of transcending the pedestrian life that so many of them live in company with other Americans.

In my view, it is because of this negative characteristic, this refusal to become non-Jews, that we see today a flourishing of Jewish religious institutions. It is true that these institutions do not evoke or engage any deep religious impulses and find their greatest strength in a weak acceptance of the mores of middle-class life. Yet they are successful only because American Jews are ready to be Jews, because they are willing to be inducted into Jewish life.

We see the reality of this readiness in the fact that to every generation of recent times a different part of the Jewish past has become meaningful. At the same time, to be sure, other parts of that tradition, great chunks without which it seemed it must die, were rejected. And yet at no point has everything been rejected at once; a kind of shifting balance has been maintained whereby each generation could relate itself meaningfully to some part of the Jewish past. It has been the course of events that has dictated which part of the Jewish past should become more prominent at any given moment— at one time, and for some Jews, it was philanthropy; at another time, and for other Jews, Zionism or Yiddish-speaking socialism; or, as today, institutional religion. The son of the Reform Jewish philanthropist who gives up the last Jewish connections his father maintained may surprise us by becoming what his father never was, a Zionist. The son of the Yiddish-speaking socialist who abandons his father's movement may join the Reform temple. In this way, each generation shoulders a minimal part of the yoke.

There are even more complex patterns than this in the maintenance of a minimal relation to Judaism. There are American Jews who have been given a good traditional education and who, following the pattern of the twenties or thirties, have broken with all religious observance. They do not attend the synagogue, they do not observe the dietary laws, they do not mark the Jewish holidays, and they do not believe in the existence of God. When this kind of Jew has children, however, he will decide that they should have some sort of Jewish education.

Such a man is not succumbing to suburban middle-class pressures; he can resist them as easily as can the classic village atheist. He may tell himself—and believe—that the children should know what it means to be a Jew, for willy-nilly they will be considered Jews and they must know how to cope with anti-Semitism. But one sees at work here that obscure process whereby a minimal relation to Judaism is established. The mental calculus seems to be as follows: Since I myself have had a good traditional education, I can afford to be an agnostic or an atheist. My child won't get such an education, but he should at least get a taste of the Jewish religion.

Philanthropy, Zionism, Jewish organizational life, attachment to Yiddish, an interest in Hasidism, a love of Hebrew, formal religious affiliation, a liking for Jewish jokes and Jewish food—none of these has, on the surface, any particularly religious meaning. Each of them reflects the concerns of the moment. The Protestant social gospel, the needs of Jews in other parts of the world, varied philosophical movements, a tendency to take pride in one's origins—each finds an echo in American Judaism. It is easy to overlook any common element in the different forms of Judaism of the different generations and see only the reflection of movements in society and thought at large. Yet what binds all these shifting manifestations of Judaism and Jewishness together is the common refusal to throw off the yoke. The refusal to become non-Jews stems from an attitude of mind that seems to be—and indeed in large measure is—a stubborn insistence on remaining a Jew, enhanced by no particularly ennobling idea of what that means. And yet it has the effect of relating

American Jews, let them be as ignorant of Judaism as a Hottentot, to a great religious tradition. Thus, the insistence of the Jews on remaining Jews, which may take the religiously indifferent forms of liking Yiddish jokes, supporting Israel, raising money for North African Jews, and preferring certain kinds of food, has a potentially religious meaning. It means that the Jewish religious tradition is not just a subject for scholars but is capable now and then of finding expression in life. And even if it finds no expression in one generation or another, the commitment to remain related to it still exists. Dead in one, two, or three generations, it may come to life in the fourth.

Or, indeed, it may not. Perhaps it is only an act of piety to preserve the relatedness to tradition. Perhaps nothing can come out of it any more, and all that remains for Jews is to act as the custodians of a museum. This is possible, too.

Yet if something were to happen, what would it be like? If the bland religious life of middle-class American Jews were to become, even to some small part of the Jewish population (we could not expect more), more alive and meaningful, what form would the change take? In the most tentative way, I would like to suggest what this form might be, by way of a description of one of the most exotic, and on the surface least significant, manifestations of Jewish religious life.

Up to now I have spoken almost entirely of what is, historically speaking, new in American Jewish life—the Reform movement, the Conservative movement, the suburban developments. I have said little of what is old—the Orthodox life of the ghettos of the big cities—because, indeed, there is little to say. It has survived—barely; and that we have said.

Today the areas of first settlement are, in all but the largest cities, deserted. The synagogues that were once churches are now churches again, or are boarded up. Negroes and Puerto Ricans now run through the corridors of settlement houses and schools in which a whole generation of Jewish business and professional men were educated. In the largest city, New York, perhaps two or three hundred thousand Jews still live in such "first settlement" neighborhoods.

The Orthodoxy of the areas of first settlement, as I have said, had almost no lasting hold on the children. As they grew up and married, they moved away—if their parents had not already moved away. If, thirty years ago, an authority had been asked to predict the future of the Lower East Side in New York and of Williamsburg in Brooklyn, he would have indicated the further decline of the Jewish population and its eventual replacement by Negroes or some new immigrant group. This is what had already happened to the neighborhoods of first Jewish settlement in smaller Jewish communities like that in Cincinnati.

In one of these areas of first settlement, however, there was a revival of an Orthodoxy of the most extreme sort that won over many of the children of the less extreme Orthodox—and even went beyond them. In Williamsburg, in Brooklyn, in a small area containing about twenty thousand people, three-quarters of them Jews, an Orthodox revival took place which, while it will never affect any but the most Orthodox fringes of American Jewry, still has something to tell us about the other variants of Jewish religious life in America.

In the middle and late thirties, the well-to-do of Williamsburg were moving out, and the half-dozen large synagogues, along with many small ones, were steadily losing members and support. A well-known and extremely Orthodox yeshiva, an all-day Jewish school for boys, and various other institutions of Orthodoxy remained. George Kranzler, writing about what happened in Williamsburg, points out that this neighborhood, undesirable to live in from almost every point of view, was attractive to Orthodox Jews because it permitted them to live a fully Jewish life as no other area did. They were willing to put up with decrepit and verminous tenement apartments, even though many could afford better elsewhere. The less Orthodox who improved their condition moved out; the more Orthodox moved in. From the late thirties on, the latter included a larger and larger proportion of refugees from Germany, Austria, Czechoslovakia, and other countries overrun by Hitler. Soon the "natives" of Williamsburg, who had prided themselves on their Orthodoxy and considered themselves the most Orthodox element in American life, found themselves outflanked by even more Orthodox elements from Europe.

But this was only the beginning. As Hitler moved into eastern Europe, he reached the area around the Carpathian Mountains where those European Jews least touched by Westernization and Western influences lived. Here Hasidism, the enthusiastic and mystical sect founded in eastern Europe in the eighteenth century, was still strong. Many of these Jews were dragged off to extermination camps. After the war, the survivors gathered in the DP camps to study the Talmud again and re-establish their communities around their surviving *rebbes*—as the leaders of the Hasidic groups are called. In the late forties, a few Hasidic *rebbes* who had settled with some followers in Williamsburg were joined by *rebbes* of much greater fame and with many more supporters. The Williamsburg norm of Orthodoxy was confirmed and heightened by this influx. The Hasidic groups established kindergartens and all-day schools for boys and girls and acquired large buildings to use as residences for their *rebbes* and as synagogues.

Up to this point, we have been describing a situation in which a particularly backward and archaic group of Jews, uprooted by war, had successfully re-established their old life in a small area. We know what (generally) happens to such ethnic enclaves: the children go to public school and one generation or at most two is enough to make ordinary Americans of them, except for those really exceptional groups like the Mennonites who are capable of resisting the larger environment.

But there is more to this particular story, and it is its most interesting part. First, Dr. Kranzler asserts, the children of this extremely Orthodox element in Williamsburg remain loyal to Orthodoxy in proportions far greater than ever before. One can partially understand this when one realizes that almost none of them goes to public school. We have here, for the first time, something that might become a Jewish equivalent of the Mennonites but with a stronger potential appeal to other Jews than the Mennonites have for other Protestants.

And, second, and this is quite unique in American Jewish religious life, the Williamsburg Hasidim have made "converts." It is true the Hasidim did not settle among Conservative or Reform or indifferent Jews; we are not dealing with a modern religious miracle. As I have said, the Jews of Williamsburg were already Orthodox before the Hasidic influx. Young, somewhat pious Williamsburg Jews would attend the services of a Hasidic *rebbe*, drawn by curiosity, and be swept up by the singing and dancing, moved by the personality of the *rebbe*, and impressed by the devotion of his followers; many would become followers themselves.

Jews from other districts would also come to see the Hasidim; on occasion—very rare occasions—a young Jew not of Orthodox background, seeking religious expression, who might in earlier years have been converted to Christianity, would visit the Hasidim and find some personal fulfilment in following their way of life. We speak of Williamsburg, because we are guided there by Dr. Kranzler's excellent study; but actually the most important of the Hasidic *rebbes* to come to America, the Lubavitcher *rebbe* who leads the Habad Hasidim, did not settle in Williamsburg. This group has had remarkable success in establishing Jewish parochial schools, not only in New York City, but in communities throughout the country, and has been most successful in attracting the interest and even allegiance of young, American-born Jews.

The reason I have described this development is not that it strikes me as a stirring in distant parts that may some day influence the whole but that it illustrates a central pattern of Jewish religious life, a pattern which I believe is somewhat distinctive, particularly as compared with what we normally expect in Christianity. The role that in Christianity is played by God's grace—operating either directly or through inspired intermediaries—is taken in Judaism by the holy community. It is that which touches and moves people, and brings them back to the faith. And the return to the faith, which in Christianity means the acceptance of beliefs—a creed, a dogma, or simply that Jesus saves—in Judaism means the return to the community, which is made holy because it lives under God's law.

The return to religion of the formerly secular-minded Yiddish writers that I spoke of in chapter vii also means the return to a community—not in this case to an actual Jewish community of today but to the community they recall from their childhood, somewhat idealized.

In Judaism, then, it is not God directly, found after an inner search, that changes man, but the example of the good and holy life, presented by the community of Jews, whether in actuality or as a historical myth or as an ideal. The disciples of the Hasidim in Williamsburg see this community before their eyes; the returning Yiddish writers recall it from the past.

But what of all the rest of American Jews, who find hardly anything attractive in either Hasidism or the Judaism of past ages, as defined by its 613 commandments? For them, the matter is far more difficult. Neither the living examples of today nor the examples of the past, of "normative" Judaism, seem viable in a modern society.

Nevertheless, the creation of examples proceeds, pragmatically and clumsily, within both the Conservative and the Reform groups. The Conservative movement struggles with the necessity of maintaining some of the practices of Orthodox Judaism, urges the use of Hebrew, speaks of the fellowship that should bind together the world-wide community of Jews. It has no desire to create a creed. Instead of depending on the attraction of a philosophy, which may convince people by reason or by giving them answers, it depends on the example of a Jewish life, which it is trying to create directly.

This is why Hebrew is so important to Conservative Judaism. What is the good, it has been asked, of taking children away for a summer to a Hebrew-speaking camp (as is done more and more frequently in the Conservative group) so that they may learn to say "Please pass the butter" in Hebrew? It makes one no more of a believer to know how to speak in Hebrew than in English. What is happening, however, is that the Conservative Jewish leaders, like the Hasidic *rebbes*, are trying to provide an example of a Jewish life so that it will not be necessary to argue and put out apologetic literature—it will only be necessary to point to a community that exists and that gives an example of what it is to be a good Jew.

In the same way, the Reform movement, once so concerned with formulating a creed, is now indifferent to that problem, but rather asks itself: What example of a Jewish life should we present, what rituals should we urge for the home, how much Hebrew should we require a Jew to know, what kind of ethical behavior should being a Jew impose on one?

Here we are, of course, very far from the Hasidim of Williamsburg, who need not ponder about what kind of Jewish life to live, though even they have certain problems in this respect. They are guided by tradition, and by leaders whose word is law. Among other Jews—and this includes Orthodox as well as Conservative and Reform Jews—the problem is the creation of a meaningful Jewish life whose power can make itself felt over those many Jews who remain, and wish to remain, open to the influence of an example. If Judaism is to become in America more than a set of religious institutions supported by a variety of social pressures, it will be by virtue of examples of Jewish lives that in some way are meaningful, that in some way permit one to be a Jew. It would be ridiculous to set up qualifications for these examples, to say that they may spring up in this or that grouping in American Jewish religious life and not in the other. What can fulfil a human life cannot be known in advance. All we can know, from the history of Judaism, is that the abstract demand to seek faith, to find God, tends to find little answer among Jews and that concrete examples of Jewish living must be given before religion has an impact on their lives. Once again, honesty requires one to say that it is possible that no satisfactory example can be given in the modern world.

IX

Epilogue: The Year 1967
and Its Meaning,
1956–72

When one considers Jewish experience in the United States in the years since 1956, one year stands out as a dividing line: 1967. The periodization of Jewish history is not the periodization of general history, nor is the periodization of American Jewish history that of American history. For the United States, the important years of this stretch of time were 1960, the election of John F. Kennedy; 1963, his assassination; 1965, the ill-fated decision to fully commit American conventional forces to the war in Vietnam; 1968, the terrible year in which both Martin Luther King and Robert F. Kennedy were assassinated.

Dates barely encompass the full reality of social developments in a period that saw an astonishing decline in American economic, political, and military power, prestige, and reputation, and an even more astonishing internal cultural revolution which reduced the country along with its institutions in the eyes of much of its intelligentsia and its youth to the level of a moral pariah.

Internally, there were two great developments during this period, and they were of great significance for American Jews. One was the increasing radicalization of American Negroes, whose preferred name changed during the decade to the more assertive "black," and many of whom shifted their political aims from integration to separation—even though the specific content and formal mechanisms of this separation were not very clear. Many blacks withdrew from—or forced whites out of—organizations in which some degree of integration had occurred (such as the political organizations fighting for civil rights), and young blacks in particular became increasingly enamored of rebellion and revolution, and the violence associated with it.

All this occurred while one social program after another was being launched to raise the economic, social, and political position of American blacks. These were almost uniformly denounced as failures by black leadership, even though there was clear evidence of rising black income, political power, and even social participation in key institutions (such as those of higher education). By the early 1970's this pattern of minority-group radicalization was being repeated among Puerto Ricans, Mexican Americans, and American Indians.

These developments had severe consequences for American Jews. Their liberal stance was challenged by its chief beneficiaries, the blacks, among whom a certain degree of annoyance with Jews and even of anti-Semitism spread. Interestingly enough, studies showed that whereas among whites in general the more educated and the younger were less anti-Semitic, among blacks the reverse was true. Inevitably, the Jewish community, which had seen much of its reason for being in its liberal political and social attitudes, began to question the value of these attitudes.

While a backlash of resistance to black political developments could be seen in the Jewish community at large, an imi-

Epilogue

tative process could be seen among Jewish youth. These asked themselves, as blacks had, whether their prosperity (much greater of course than that of blacks) had been bought at the price of the surrender of distinctive spiritual and cultural values. Just as young blacks had turned on their established leaders, so, too, now did many young Jews. Just as young blacks found their leadership too accommodative to American political reality, so, too, did many young Jews. Even black rhetoric was copied. Blacks denounced their "Uncle Toms," and Jews in imitation denounced their "Uncle Jakes," as they dubbed the established leaders who reasoned and bargained with the non-Jewish powers instead of—in the new favored style—demanding and threatening.

A second major development, with perhaps even more significant impact on American Jews during these years, was the astonishing growth of political and cultural radicalism among the youth. In the late 1950's, American youth was regularly seen by analysts of American society as conventional and conforming: concerned with achieving a good middle-class status, a secure job, a family, a home, involved in its private concerns and uninterested in the larger world, which it was happy to leave to the management of its elders. In those days, the special publications addressed to youth were written by adults who were interested in selling them products; the music to which youth listened and danced was written by the professionals of the popular music industry; youth's dress was not markedly different from that of adults, and was dominated by the adult fashion industry.

A totally unexpected youth rebellion which altered all this beyond recognition marked the latter half of the 1960's. Perhaps the first harbinger was the rise of a special youth music, written by youth, which achieved worldwide impact with the Beatles. "We are now more popular than Jesus," said one Beatle on a triumphal tour of the United States. Indeed, it was not long before any effort to make Jesus popular among American youth seemed to require casting him in a rock opera and fitting him out with the music, hair styles, speech, and clothing of the Beatles and their successors.

Quite independently of these cultural developments, a youth rebellion broke out in political form in the idyllic setting of the University of California at Berkeley in 1964. The Berkeley "Free Speech Movement" used the language forged in old movements against repression, but it was soon clear that it was directed against a new enemy, industrial society itself, a society which promised ease but expected conformity and discipline. A new language justifying rebellion against a non-repressive society was forged. The real historical novelty of the Berkeley rebellion—which was perhaps the first rebellion in history by the most favored elements of a free society, rather than by the least favored of a repressive one—was soon obscured by America's massive entry into the Vietnam war. This meant that, along with the novelty, which persisted, much more traditional politically radical groups and theories were resuscitated and incorporated into the youth rebellion. Thus, alongside those who urged non-violence, spiritual renewal, a new culture, and the re-creation of a sense of community, there arose groups of radicals who revived the doctrines of Marx, Trotsky, Stalin, Rosa Luxemburg, and even more obscure revolutionaries and, astonishingly enough, found substantial American followers for these doctrines as well as those of Castro and Mao.

The cultural and political rebellions were at times fused, at times separate. A whole new youth "counterculture" emerged.

Epilogue

The colleges and universities—which increasing numbers of American youth entered during the 1960's—shook under the impact of the revolution. College presidents were toppled from the leading institutions of American higher education, and not college presidents alone. President Johnson, as well as a near-president, Hubert Humphrey, may be seen in part as victims of the youth rebellion. Inevitably, this was to have great impact on American Jews, for their children attended colleges in numbers far greater than other Americans and were more susceptible to radical political thought than other Americans.

The years since 1956, then, suggest to us a profile of American developments in which an early peaking of American hopes for change and progress internally and in international relations, between 1961 and 1964, was followed by steady decline after 1965. But the profile of internal American Jewish developments was quite the reverse. The postwar excitement over a "Jewish revival" came to an end in the late 1950's. Interest in Jewish religion and in Jewish issues among young Jews seemed to have reached a nadir in the early 1960's. But in the latter part of the decade, one overwhelming event, the Israeli war of 1967 and its consequences, transformed the scene, leading Jews to a new intensity of self-consciousness and a new level of concern for Jewish issues, among them religious issues.

In 1956 American Judaism was in the full flush of what was called a Jewish revival. Those of theological or deeply religious inclination would not have used this term. There was no great revival of interest in Jewish tradition, of Jewish religious practice, of Jewish education. There was no flowering of Jewish sages and philosophers, or of Jewish piety. What was happening was that synagogues and temples were being built in large numbers, particularly in the new suburban neighborhoods into which newly prosperous Jewish businessmen and professionals were moving. Jewish children were attending part-time Jewish schools under congregational auspices in ever larger numbers. Most Jews were becoming members of such congregations. Money was raised for the new congregations and schools and for the support of the central seminaries in which rabbis were trained.

But there was a deep dissatisfaction among the religiously inclined, who argued that all this had a purely "social" meaning. They meant that Jews, despite their higher education, their greater prosperity, their entry into upper middle-class occupations, still seemed to prefer association with other Jews in Jewish social circles. These circles in turn inevitably supported Jewish religious institutions, as I explain in chapter vii. Involvement in Jewish religious institutions was, in the new suburbs, the chief way in which Jews came in touch with Jewish social circles. Jewish religious institutions thus existed to further Jewish social life. Jews still insisted on Jewish identification for their children and found they could get it through Jewish education, or at least hoped they could. At the same time, parents resisted intensive and "too Jewish" an education—another indication that the Jewish revival was more social than religious.

How could this social religion be interpreted? One interpretation—and it seemed the most persuasive—was that, while America was still organized in large part into ethnic enclaves and ethnic organizations, ethnicity denoted working-class status and recent arrival, and carried with it as well the color of an inadequate or insufficient Americanization. For middle-class people of the second and third generation in America, the maintenance of social ties through ethnic social organization seemed inappropriate. Religious organization, on the other hand, was completely American, fully accepted, legitimate, and suffered no color of foreignness. Religious forms thus became a convenient shell for an ethnic social content.

While this seemed true enough, it could also be argued—as I argue in chapter viii—that the identification with religious institutions, even in the absence of any extensive knowledge of Jewish religion or any extensive practice of Jewish religious requirements, had a religious meaning. This meaning was to be found in "the refusal to become non-Jews," and it was religiously significant because of the unbreakable and yet not easily comprehensible tie between the Jewish people and the Jewish religion. The fact is, Judaism was the religion of a people. Without Jews, it was inconceivable that there could be Judaism. It was not a religion that sought converts, though there were converts to Judaism (almost entirely it must be said because of marriage to a Jew: "conversion" was thus a way of joining the Jewish people rather than the Jewish religion!). It was not a religion that spread its message disinterestedly before all peoples, as did Buddhism, Islam, Christianity. Without Jews there might be Jewish scholarship; there could not be a living Judaism.

Where were the strains in this comfortable arrangement? Why could not Jews continue as a people under the guise of a religion? One strain arose from the triple split within American Judaism. Orthodoxy upheld the traditional religion with as few changes as one could manage, and in the case of extreme Orthodoxy, none. Reform specifically repealed the traditional basis of Judaism, the Jewish law as developed and interpreted in the Talmud and subsequently, and asserted that reason was capable, with only limited assistance from tradition, of defining a religious stance in the modern world. Conservatism led an uneasy existence between the two, but one in which, for this reason alone, the tensions within contemporary Judaism were best exposed. While the Protestant denominations in the United States went through a steady process of merger during the 1950's and 1960's, a process which recognized the reduction of religious differences between them, and while the Second Vatican Council of 1961–64 led to increasing dialogue between Catholics and Protestants, the Jewish "branches" (a term which better characterizes the three groups than "denomination") seemed to find it increasingly difficult to overcome their differences.

In particular, Orthodoxy, even though it had become the smallest of the branches, was the most aggressive. Presumably this self-confidence was drawn from the fact that it most closely followed the tradition and thus had the least to explain or to ponder in its adaptation to the modern world. Undoubtedly this self-confidence was also sustained by the fact that the Judaism of the state of Israel—and the only form of Judaism recognized there—was the same as Orthodoxy in America. This meant that while American Orthodox rabbis were considered by Israeli religious authorities part of a body of properly authorized religious functionaries capable of performing marriages, divorces, and conversions, Conservative and Reform rabbis were not. Despite the long and strong association of the Conservative and Reform rabbinate and congregations and seminaries with Israel, they were forced to accept an inferior status in Israel.

Orthodox vigor was best shown in its day-school movement. Whereas the great majority of Jewish children who attended Jewish schools attended either a Sunday school (42 per cent in 1966–67) meeting one day a week, or an afternoon school meet-

ing two or more days a week (44 per cent in 1966–67), 13 per-
cent attended private schools under Jewish religious auspices
in which they received both secular and religious instruction,
and these were overwhelmingly Orthodox. The all-day school
had in time been adopted by the Conservatives—Rabbi Robert
Gordis founded the first one in 1951—and by 1971 even the
Reform group was beginning to establish day schools.

Jewish thinkers were deeply troubled by one aspect of this
threefold split: the growing refusal of Orthodox elements to
recognize Conservative and Reform rabbis. Would this not
inevitably mean a basic split in the Jewish people? Would not
the status of Jews involved in the marriages, divorces, and conversions carried out by Reform and Conservative rabbis become ambiguous? While young Jewish thinkers from each
group found more and more in common, the branches as a
whole—in their formal institutional role—seemed to find it
impossible to overcome those aspects of their divisions that presented serious consequences for the Jewish people. Rabbi Jakob
J. Petuchowski raised the point most effectively:

"The Covenant at Sinai was made 'with him who is standing
here with us this day before the Lord our God, and also with
him who is not here this day' (Deuteronomy 29:14). Tradition
knows of two ways in which one becomes a Jew. One is either
born into the Covenant Community, and thus acquires his status
by virtue of the Covenant (made also 'with him who is not here
this day'); or one can come into Judaism from the outside by
undergoing the accepted rites of conversion. Once one is a Jew,
he may turn out to be a good Jew, or a bad Jew, or a sinful
Jew; but his 'Jewishness' itself cannot be called into question.
This . . . can work only so long as the whole Covenant Community is in agreement on the marriage law in terms of which

a 'Jewish birth' takes place, and on the details of the conversion procedure by means of which outsiders are accepted into the field.

"It is thus the Jewish law concerning 'personal status' which guarantees the underlying unity of the 'holy community.' But it is precisely the legislation concerning 'personal status' (and the requirements for conversion) which Reform Jews, particularly in America, have largely chosen to ignore. They have thereby provoked some Orthodox rabbis (and the government of the State of Israel) into rejecting the validity of Jewish marriages performed under Reform Jewish auspices.

"The fault, however, is not all on one side. The traditional Jewish marriage and divorce law is predicated on a status of women in society which no longer corresponds to the actual status of women in the modern world. There are, therefore, changes which will have to be made in Jewish marriage and divorce law, even as changes have always been made before in the millennial development of the Tradition. The Orthodox rabbinate has been remiss in making those changes. . . .

"In this process, a division is being created in the 'holy community,' a division which, in succeeding generations, is bound to lead to many cases of hardship and personal tragedy. It is also a growing rift which threatens the underlying unity of all Jews. And once that underlying unity disappears, the present religious pluralism may well turn into complete religious anarchy; and total religious anarchy may spell the end of the Covenant Community, in which alone Judaism as a faith can have its being and significance."[1]

This rather esoteric cause of concern about the future of the Jewish people—whatever its ultimate significance—affected mostly rabbis and theologians. A second cause of concern was more widespread and became particularly strong in the 1960's.

Epilogue

This was fear that the number of Jews was declining, through simple failure to reproduce and through intermarriage. Articles in the *American Jewish Year Book* regularly reported on the extent of intermarriage, size of Jewish population, birth rate. It was difficult to give determinative answers because of the continuing failure of the United States census to ask a question on religion (in part because of pressure from Jewish organizations who felt it would be unwise to gather official statistics on religion). Some studies—particularly one in the city of Washington and one in the state of Indiana—came up with remarkably high rates of intermarriage. Intermarriage was particularly high in the third generation and among the better educated. And as Jews became better educated—and they were achieving phenomenally high levels of education, to the point where continuing beyond the B.A. to graduate education was very common among them—and as they became more and more removed from their immigrant and Orthodox origins, would not the intermarriage rate increase?[2] Intermarriage rates had been very high in Germany, Austria, and Hungary between the wars. Were not the Jews of the United States, through low birth rate and intermarriage, assuring their eventual disappearance? The proportion of Jews in the American population, by best estimate, seemed to have declined from 3.7 per cent of the population in 1937 to 2.9 per cent in 1968.[3] This may on the surface hardly appear a religious concern, but as a matter of fact the link between the Jewish people and Judaism, as I have pointed out, assures that it will be. The subject of the dangers of intermarriage was always sure to draw a substantial audience at a Jewish synagogue or temple, which was evidence that the members were concerned not only with the opportunities for Jewish social life today but also that their children should maintain a Jewish identity and Jewish community in the future.

American Judaism

By the end of the 1960's, some of these fears were moderated. It turned out that while indeed many Jews married non-Jews, many of the spouses were converted and many of the children of these marriages were raised as Jews. According to one study in Providence, Rhode Island, the net result was a gain in Jewish population. Nor, in Providence, did the third generation show a particularly high rate of intermarriage; and it had more children than the second generation. The picture was mixed, but the Jew in America was not physically disappearing.

The discussion of such issues leads us to a third major concern of Jews in the 1960's, a concern which had existed since a substantial part of the Jewish people had turned from the traditional law, and this was the issue of "survivalism." By this Jews meant the interest of Jews in surviving as Jews, with no additional interest in what the *content* of Jewish life and religion should be. Was not the Jewish religion itself pressed into the service of mere survival, since so many Jews identified with synagogues and temples not because of concern for religion but because they wanted to stay with Jews, to strengthen the Jewish causes and communal life, and to ensure that their children married Jews—all pure "survivalist" aims?

And this brings us to the fourth and final issue we will raise as troublesome for Judaism in the 1960's, and that was the issue of community. The new synagogues and temples were often denounced as "soulless." Members of the older generation, who recalled the smaller, more informal, more personalistic and communal synagogues of their youth, found them so. More important, perhaps, Jewish youth found them so. The great majority of American Jewish youth refused to participate in Jewish communal or religious life. Most Jews on the campuses rarely attended religious services, and only minuscule numbers supported Jewish institutions, such as Hillel and student Zionist organizations. Jewish observers asked, Did not Jewish youth fail to identify with Jewish organizations and the Jewish community primarily because these failed to give youth the heightened and valid sense of community it sought? The experience of the decades of the twenties and thirties suggested that these young people who were completely uninterested in Judaism would later become affiliated as they married and had children and developed their own "survivalist" concerns, but was this enough?

In the preceding chapter, written in the middle 1950's, I referred to such visible evidences and experiences of community as that given by the Hasidim and to experiments such as the Conservative Hebrew-speaking camps that were trying to provide an aspect of communal experience to contemporary youth. A number of writers considered how a more tangible communal dimension might be provided in Jewish religious life. Rabbi Petuchowski, in 1960, was perhaps the first to use the term *havurah*, "fellowship" or "brotherhood," and to suggest that there might be models in Jewish history that could be followed to intensify the sense of community:

"One is the 'Covenant' (*amanah*) in the days of Ezra, entered into by the exiles returning from Babylon. In the account of that 'Covenant' there is a verse which can be helpful to us in our present predicament: 'We also lay upon ourselves *mitzvoth*.' Those *mitzvoth*, or obligations, are spelled out in some detail. They all have to do with the self-preservation of the small group of returning exiles, who obligated themselves to maintain the sanctuary and its cult, to observe the Sabbath, and to reject mixed marriages.

"The precise details do not matter so much in our particular context. What does matter is the fact of the *voluntary* acceptance of Jewish obligations on the part of the people, the 'self-imposed' authority behind the standard of observance. This could well serve as a precedent for our own acceptance of certain obligations, of certain *mitzvoth* which are ours to perform, not so much because they represent God's Word to us individually, but because they represent the 'constitution' of the 'holy community.'

"But if that precedent, set by the people as a whole, and under circumstances quite different from our own, can no longer be imitated by us in a slavish manner, there yet remains one other precedent in our history which has a very direct relevance to our latter-day problem. We are referring to the *chabhuroth*, the Pharisaic 'brotherhoods,' organized in the days of the Second Temple. Those 'brotherhoods' were formed by Jews who made a number of 'ritual' laws more stringent for themselves, and who became more particular and meticulous in the laws governing tithing and levitical purity than was the current Jewish practice of their time. The 'brotherhoods,' as *voluntary* associations, maintained their own superior standards, and they did have very rigorous 'entrance requirements.'

"The exclusivism of the Pharisaic 'brotherhoods,' their 'setting themselves apart' from the rest of the people, may indicate a tendency at variance with the lowest common denominator which, in our own days, is all too often elevated as the 'democratic' standard. But it remains to be pointed out that, ultimately, those elite groups set the standards for the people as a whole. Their particular interpretation of the Torah gained virtually universal acceptance, and the very stringency of their 'ritual' observance, which they adopted as the badge of their exclusiveness, became, in the course of time, the *norm* of Jewish piety for everyone alike."[4]

Epilogue

Jacob Neusner, a young scholar who was engaged in a monumental study of the Jewish community of "Babylonia" (Sassanid Mesopotamia) from which the Talmud had emerged and who saw parallels between the Jewish community there and the Jewish community of the contemporary United States (in both, Jews were free to develop in an ethnically pluralist society), also wrote about the possibilities of the "fellowship" as a form for Jewish life:

"The fellowship in ancient times rested on the ideal of commonwealth, the sense that some men actually had common concerns and commitments which might be articulated through that particular institution. If there is in the end no underlying community in which men actually participate and for which they care, the fellowship is a useless device. From this viewpoint, however, one finds some slender hope: the Jews do seem to choose to remain a group, as the existence of Jewish neighbourhoods, hotels, fraternities, and the synagogues themselves testify. If this choice is a negative one, its consequences do not have to be negative. One can attempt to transform a group which finds its definition by contrast to the 'outside world' into a group which is constituted on affirmative inward social experience. Even today the Jews continue to manifest certain qualities of a fellowship; if not in a given synagogue, then in a given town, they do acknowledge their fellowship in some ways. One might well criticize the expressions of that fellowship, but one cannot ignore its presence in American cities. Attenuated ties bind Jews into an attenuated community. On this basis one may hope to recover the reality of fellowship and community."[5]

It was hardly likely that these or other suggestions in the relatively rarefied worlds of Jewish scholarship, theology, and religious discussion would have much direct impact on the major Jewish religious institutions, let alone the masses of Jews whose relationship to these institutions was as passive members and financial supporters rather than as involved participants. Nor did the Jewish religious institutions find it necessary to respond to the ending, in the early 1960's, of the long sustained expansion of the synagogues and temples. The steady increase in membership came to an end in the early 1960's. Enrolment in Jewish schools hit its peak in 1962, when 589,000 students were recorded. In 1966–67 the figure had dropped to 554,000. (On the other hand, the number in day schools, as I have pointed out, largely Orthodox but some Conservative, continued to rise.) The expansion of Jewish congregations and schools had paralleled the Jewish movement to suburbia. There came a time when this movement inevitably slowed down. In many cities (for example, Cleveland), there was hardly a Jewish population by the early 1960's—everyone had moved off to the suburbs. When each suburb had a Reform, Conservative, and Orthodox congregation, opportunities for expansion in the number of new synagogues and temples were limited. The reduction in Jewish school enrolments was a different matter, but since those seriously interested in Jewish education thought very poorly of Sunday schools and limited afternoon schools, and since it was among these the reduction occurred, it did not create great concern among the religiously oriented.

In the first half of the sixties, aside from these religious issues, there were no areas in which American Jews had any immediate problems. The prosperity of the Jewish community continued. I have pointed out how studies around 1950 (pp. 107–8) recorded the decline in the Jewish working class and the increase in the number of white-collar workers, proprietors and managers, and professionals. In the 1960's the numbers in the higher

Epilogue

non-manual occupations increased yet further. Thus, studies in New York City (1963–64), Boston (1965), Milwaukee (1964–65), and Springfield, Massachusetts (1966), record high percentages, between 22 and 32, of professionals among all male Jews employed. Between 25 and 39 per cent of all male Jews were proprietors and managers. Clerical and sales workers in the four cities made up between 19 and 31 per cent of the male working population. In New York City there was still a substantial number of Jewish manual workers—23 per cent of all employed Jewish males—but for males in the other cities, which were typical of American Jewish communities outside New York, the percentages ranged between 8.5 and 15.[6]

Nor was there much concern over anti-Semitism in the first half of the 1960's. Anti-Semitism seemed to have become almost invisible. The main interests of the Jewish defense organizations were the Vatican Council's statement on the Jews, the few remaining pockets of discrimination in the higher reaches of corporations, the enhancing of Jewish identity, and—most important—the general area of civil rights legislation, administration, and adjudication, in which Jewish organizations, with their substantial staffs and budgets and their political knowledge and connections, played an important role.

But internal developments were soon to change the placid domestic scene. While Martin Luther King, Roy Wilkins, James Farmer of the Congress of Racial Equality, and the nonviolent and religiously inclined student leaders of the Student Nonviolent Coordinating Committee were the domiant figures in the Negro civil rights movement—as they were until 1965—Jewish groups and individuals worked closely with them. In 1965 the slogan "Black Power" was raised. It could mean many things. But one thing it meant was that, compared with the summer of 1964 when hundreds of white youths (largely Jewish) poured into Mississippi to work against white racism under black auspices, the white role in SNCC—very soon in CORE, too—rapidly declined. Soon whites were not welcome, except as contributors of funds or as lawyers, often defending blacks against charges stemming from the new turn to violence. Starting in 1964 and continuing through 1968, massive summer riots by blacks occurred in American cities. Jewish storekeepers suffered severely, and this began to put a strain on Jewish sympathies for civil rights, as well as to arouse new fears for the Jewish position. Everywhere in the later 1960's one saw a renewal of black pride. The blacks insisted now that "black was beautiful," and blacks must "do their own thing." On campuses from about 1968 whites were shocked as black students demanded separate housing quarters, separate centers for their activities, all-black classes barred to whites.

In 1964, the white student movement suddenly sprang to prominence. The Students for a Democratic Society had been organizing, attracting little notice, in white and black sections of northern cities. Now they found a new constituency on the campuses. Simultaneously, they began to move away from nonviolence. Just as young blacks rejected the influence of Martin Luther King, white radical students, too, began to find revolutionary doctrines and violence more attractive. The two movements were parallel but rarely worked together, because the black movement had as its basic requirement an insistence on its own independent community, its independent structures uninfluenced by the white world, radical or liberal. And yet, working along these independent lines, both movements discovered Marxism and revolutionary doctrines, and were attracted to them.

Epilogue

There is hardly any evidence that the many young Jews who had been so prominent in the civil rights movement (of the three martyrs of Philadelphia, Mississippi, in the summer of 1964, the two whites were Jews), or who were so prominent in the radical student movement that grew in the wake of the Berkeley student uprising and the American intervention in Vietnam, thought of themselves as Jews rather than students or reformers. Hardly anyone else thought of them as Jews, either. Jews were numerous on college campuses. While they formed only 3 per cent of the population, it was a rare campus of intellectual distinction on which Jews did not constitute 15 or 20 per cent of the student body. They were more numerous than that in the radical movement, which in its first years was restricted to the elite and larger campuses. Many of the Jewish students had, after all, come from socialist and communist families, and whatever their rebellion against society, studies showed they were not rebelling against their families. But in 1967 something happened that suddenly sharpened their consciousness of being Jews as well as radicals and led to a remarkable change of position by many of them.

What happened was the ominous threat to Israel that grew during the spring until the agonizing days of May when the Egyptian and other armies organized against Israel and when it seemed to most observers that inevitably Israel must be overwhelmed by Arab armies lavishly equipped by Communist Russia. Why did this event have such a powerful impact on American Jews? While American Jews supported Israel, their support for many years had not been fervent. The sums they contributed each year remained constant. Young Zionists were hard to find. To the disappointment of Israeli leaders, young American Jews had never shown much interest in going to

Israel. More Israelis emigrated to the United States than young American Jews emigrated to Israel. In addition, by 1967 the college youth—and certainly the Jews among them—strongly opposed the Vietnam war, and any American commitment overseas. Many young persons saw every such commitment as imperialistic, and all those countries who accepted such a commitment as puppets or satellites or colonies or imperialist exploiters themselves.

And yet we must record that American Jews, among them even the Jewishly indifferent youth whose energies had for so long been engaged by the cause of the Negroes or the poor or the Vietnamese, suddenly discovered that the fate of Israel, of Jews of different language, culture, and state, meant more to them than these other causes.

It is hard to document a sudden reversal of feeling. Yet everyone who lived through it has attested to it, and perhaps the most persuasive evidence is that given by young Jewish leftists themselves, who wrote and reported and recorded what the terrible danger of extermination through which Israel had lived had meant to them. They were surprised and astonished by their own depth of feeling. A good part of the literature of Jewish youth after 1967—the literature to be found in many Jewish student newspapers founded after 1969, the pages of *Response*, a magazine founded in that summer of 1967, and elsewhere— refers back to those days of 1967 as a turning point. Writing in the *American Jewish Year Book, 1968*, Rabbi Arthur Hertzberg summed it up:

"The immediate reaction of American Jewry to the crisis was far more intense and widespread than anyone could have foreseen. Many Jews would never have believed that the grave danger to Israel would dominate their thoughts and emotions

Epilogue

to the exclusion of all else." And Lucy S. Dawidowicz, in a full and convincing documentation of the response of young Jews in the same issue of the *Year Book*, writes that many "found [that] their ideas of war, which had been shaped by Vietnam, were irrelevant to Israel. Views on pacifism, civil disobedience, resistance to government, and the inherent evil of military might were suddenly questioned."[7] Jewish radicals who were involved in the movement of the New Left, such as Irving Louis Horowitz and Martin Peretz, documented the great impact the Israeli war had on the Jews in the movement.

But why did the war have such an impact on American Jews, when the Arab-Jewish war of 1956, for example, seemed to have had no particular impact at all? In the middle 1950's, indeed, it appeared that the establishment of the state of Israel had not affected American Jews very much (see chapter viii, p. 115).

There were three reasons for this enormous impact of the 1967 war, and all require some discussion. One was the growing emotional response among American Jews to the Holocaust of 1939–45. A second was the response of black and white radical groups in the United States to the position of Israel. A third was the distinctive role of Russia, the home of the second largest community of Jews in the world, as the chief big-power enemy of Israel. Each of these facts emphasized the overwhelming *aloneness* of the Jews. Each of them emphasized the peculiar *distinctiveness* of the Jews. Each of them justified to Jews, as nothing had for the entire period between 1945 and 1967, and to the young who had not seen themselves as Jews, the right to consider themselves specially threatened and specially worthy of whatever efforts were necessary for survival. Inevitably, such a viewpoint had or could have a religious meaning.

Just as, writing in the mid-fifties, I could see no specific major impact of the state of Israel on the internal life of American Jews, I could see no specific major impact of the Holocaust (see chapter viii, pp. 114–15). After 1967 this was no longer true. During the 1960's American Jews subtly became more sensitized to the enormity of the extermination of the Jews. The Israeli action in kidnapping, trying, and executing Adolf Eichmann in 1961 had some effect in getting Jews to think about the Holocaust. One can hardly avoid psychoanalytic language. These events had been repressed, not only among American Jews but among many of the survivors themselves, hundreds of thousands of whom had settled in the United States. Eichmann's trial made it impossible to repress the events any longer. Hannah Arendt's assessment of the events, which she covered for the *New Yorker* magazine and in her book, *Eichmann in Jerusalem* (New York: Viking Press, 1963), in which modern society in general and Jewish communal leadership specifically seemed to emerge as principal villains in the case, unnerved many Jews and was passionately attacked. Meanwhile Elie Wiesel's direct and unsparing books on the extermination camps, combined with his own commitment to the Jewish fate, also began to lead Jews to confront these overwhelming events.

It can scarcely be suggested that *many* Jews were affected by this reawakening of the impact of the Holocaust before 1967. Indeed, when *Commentary* addressed a series of questions on Jewish belief to a large group of young Jewish religious thinkers and writers in 1966, the Holocaust did not figure among the questions, nor, it must be said, did it figure much among the answers (*The Condition of Jewish Belief*, edited by Milton Himmelfarb [New York: Macmillan, 1966]). Before 1967, young radical Jews were quite capable of using the term "genocide" to describe what was happening to American Negroes or Vietnamese, with no self-consciousness of the fact that their own people had truly been subject, and recently, to a not wholly unsuccessful effort to kill them all. Suddenly, 1967 raised sharply the possibility of real genocide again. Arab spokesmen promised it. The example of Jews being killed while the world stood by was already present in recent history. And in 1967 the world stood by, and Israel was quite clearly alone.

That the United States should talk, that France should caution, that England should follow the American lead, and that Russia was actively supporting the enemies of Israel—all this was bad enough. But young radical Jews were suddenly aware that those with whom they had fought and worked, black militants and New Leftists, were also enemies of Israel. The summer ghetto riots after 1964 had been accompanied by a certain amount of anti-Semitism. Now black militants began to combine domestic anti-Semitism with international anti-Zionism. For various reasons, black militants tended to identify with Islam and with the Arab states. To them 1967 was a "Zionist imperialist war."

Shortly after the 1967 war, one of the largest gatherings of the various groups loosely associated in the New Left met in Chicago in a Convention for a New Politics. As was inevitably the case with such meetings, a large part of the attendance was of Jewish leftists, as was much of the financial backing that made the convention possible. The blacks at the meeting insisted that the convention pass a resolution condemning the "Zionist imperialist" war. This was the breaking point for many Jewish leftists.

Meanwhile, white radical groups on the left, in the course of developing their ideology as to the distinctive role of the United

States (often dubbed "Amerika") as the source of all evil in the world, inevitably denounced Israel, too. While those most active in the denunciation of Israel were Jews (as was almost inevitable, in view of the Jewish prominence in left-wing groups in the United States), many other Jews dissociated themselves in anger and disgust.

The internal developments in the black and white left had one other effect in shaping the Jewish response to Israel. Black self-assertion, now being copied by other groups in the United States, for many Jews legitimated Jewish self-assertion. It was not easy for any group of Americans simply to insist that their homelands or the countries with which they were associated should be defended by the United States independently of the interests of the United States. Some Jews had always been troubled by the problem of dual loyalty. But the legitimation of the assertion of the validity of distinctive group interests, which was one result of the black revolution, made it easier for Jews, too, directly to support the interests of Israel, and for young Jews on the campuses to support Jewish interests. The black example should not be underestimated in explaining why young Jews turned inward and became active supporters of what they now conceived of as Jewish interests, rather than embarrassed rejecters of the validity of such interests.

Finally, the international role of the left also served to awaken young Jews to the special danger to Israel. Communist Russia—generally seen in the New Left as bureaucratic and without revolutionary vigor—provided arms to the Arabs. But Communist China, admired in the New Left, provided arms and support for the most extreme of the Arab guerrilla groups, the one most active in claiming credit for such outrageous acts as the killing of Jewish schoolchildren. And Communist Cuba, most widely admired in the New Left, also supported the Arabs. Thus young Jews who were more or less influenced by the New Left had to confront directly the conflict between any Jewish feeling they possessed and the uniform hostility of the Communists in all countries to the Israelis. In this confrontation, many discovered in themselves more Jewish feeling than they had suspected.

We must note too the special impact on young Jews of the situation of Jews in Russia and Eastern Europe. In the wake of 1967, a new wave of anti-Semitism (called anti-Zionism) swept Poland, where the pitiful remnants of what had been one of the largest Jewish communities in the world were forced out of their jobs and into emigration. In the wake of the 1967 war, Russia's anti-Zionist propaganda campaign reached new extremes of violence and irrationality, as the Israelis were regularly denounced for "Hitlerite" acts. Young Jews became aware of the three million Jews who lived in Russia and were far more deprived of rights than the Negroes whose cause the young American Jews had so long supported. The organized Jewish community had for some years been trying to develop public pressure over the problem of the Jews of Russia, who were deprived of the right to practice their religion and culture freely, who could not associate with Jews outside Russia, could not express their sympathy with Israel, and could not emigrate. After 1967 young Jews took up the issue. Unfortunately some of them began to apply the militant tactics that had been made popular by young blacks and New Leftists, disrupting concerts of visiting Russian artists, harassing Russian representatives, on occasion even planting bombs and attempting hijackings. In particular a "Jewish Defense League," organized in the poorer, Orthodox, working-class sections of New York and other large cities, engaged in the more obnoxious tactics. But for the most part the young Jews concerned with Soviet Jewry eschewed such tactics.

After 1967, three different positions were to be found among young Jews who were concerned with Jewish issues. Some still identified almost completely with the New Left and attempted to develop a distinctive Jewish orientation within it which would nevertheless share the New Left's criticism of Israel as an exemplar of social injustice and as a protégé of an imperialistic United States. The main thrust of these groups seemed to be to demonstrate to the militant blacks and other radical elements that Jews, too, could be radical in a Jewish way. Jews for Urban Justice and Arthur Waskow represented this tendency.

But on the issue of Israel specifically, other groups of Jewish New Leftists broke away. One such group founded a Jewish student newspaper, the *Jewish Radical*, in Berkeley in 1969. Within two years there were nearly forty more Jewish student newspapers established in almost every center in which there were large numbers of Jewish students, with more being founded. These newspapers identified themselves with three causes. One was Israel. Though many remained critical of its internal policies and in particular its policies toward the Arabs in Israel and the occupied territories, all insisted on Israel's right to exist and defend itself. A second was Soviet Jewry and its right to cultural and religious freedom and emigration. A third was the state of the American Jewish community, which they criticized for support of American foreign policies, for failure adequately to support Jewish education, for in effect "selling out" to America by becoming middle class and patriotic.

The institutions of the Jewish community, delighted to see

any concern with Jewish affairs among the youth, were generally happy to support these newspapers, even if the Jewish community itself, its fund-raising and defense organizations, its synagogues and temples, were one of the chief targets of the newspapers.

Finally, aside from the groups closely associated with the New Left, and those who disengaged themselves from it as the hostility of black and white radicals to Israel persisted, there was yet a third group of young Jews who were leftist only to the extent that most of their generation were and who were concerned with Jewish religious issues specifically. This group also adopted as its chief causes Israel, Soviet Jewry, and the state of the Jewish community. But it was the last that concerned it most: the weakness of Jewish education, the lack of fervor of Jewish religious practice, the failure to develop a real "community" within the American Jewish community. Among their favored terms—true also of the rest of their generation— were authenticity and commitment. This group was best exemplified by the editors and writers of the magazine *Response*, and it was among them that the experiments in fellowship and brotherhood proposed years before by Petuchowski and Neusner found expression in the formation of communities devoted to study, the *havurah*s of Boston and New York. These are perhaps best described as small informal seminaries, but they shared some of the motivations and ideologies of the communes that were springing up all over America, in particular their insistence on close personal relations and a spirit of true community.

In my discussion of the response to 1967, I have concentrated on the young Jews, because their reaction was the most surprising. But the response among the older generation and among the thinkers and theologians was also deep and unexpected. As Rabbi Richard Rubenstein wrote, "I can report that many Jews who had imagined themselves to be totally devoid of any inner connection with Jewish life were overwhelmed by their involvement in Israel's trial. . . . I must confess surprise over the depth of my own feelings. There are unconscious depths to the phenomenon of Jewishness which even those of us who have spent our lives in its study cannot fathom. No Jewish theology will be adequate which fails to take account of the response of the world's Jews to Israel's recent struggle."[8]

We will leave for later the significant last sentence of this quotation, and consider for the moment the more mundane responses of American Jews. Impressive was the huge outpouring of money. In 1966, $64 million was raised for Israel, and $76 million in Israel Bonds were sold. In 1967 contributions quadrupled, to $242 million; bond sales increased two and a half times, to $190 million, for an astonishing total of $432 million raised voluntarily from the American Jewish community (which numbered under six million) in one year. In the next year, contributions continued far above the 1966 rate, to reach $155 million; and bond sales, too, were far higher than before the war, $107 million. A new plateau of giving for Israel had been established.

More striking to my mind than the increase in financial contributions was the beginning, for the first time since the founding of Israel, of substantial American Jewish emigration to Israel. "In 1966," writes George E. Gruen, "the total number of Americans in Israel was probably somewhere between 12,000 and 15,000. Since 1967, almost 17,000 new American immigrants settled in Israel. . . . Moreover, the figures represent a sharply rising trend:

Epilogue

1967	1,700
1968	4,300
1969	6,700
1970	9,200

"In fact, last year [1970], the United States, for the first time in Israel's history, surpassed all other countries as the single source of immigration."[9] One must add to this the fact that young American Jews, without any marked Jewish interest, travel now in great numbers to Israel to experience Israeli life at first hand.

Events in Israel, combined with domestic developments, led to a more troubled examination of the Jewish conscience than American Jews had been accustomed to for more than twenty years. American Jews defined themselves generally as liberals. This meant they supported Negro civil rights, civil liberties, looked benignly on left-wing causes, supported self-determination, national liberation movements, and anti-colonialism, were critical of the size of the American military establishment and the direction of American foreign policy, and were strongly opposed to intervention in Vietnam. But at the same time they were Jews, and they found that their powerful instinctive support of Israel was opposed by many of their almost equally instinctive political commitments. How could they reconcile their criticisms of the American role in Vietnam with their demand that America support Israel? I do not say that such a reconciliation was not possible—I believe it was—but the fact is that it had to be *attempted*, and in attempting it many Jews were driven to adopt, on other issues, a less liberal position. They were not perhaps as critical of the American role in Vietnam anymore, or of the American armed forces; they became more critical of the Communist countries and the varied "national liberation movements" that seemed so hostile to Israel. They became more critical of the militant American blacks who opposed Israel.

Of course this development toward a more conservative position could not be ascribed only to the crisis of Israel. Domestic developments, too, were pushing American Jews in this direction. As the long-delayed efforts at integration of the public schools finally made an impact on northern cities, Jews found that they were not eager to send their children to black inner-city schools, even though they had for so long fervently supported integration. Those wealthier Jews who lived in all-white or largely white suburbs could still support integration. Less prosperous Jews in the central cities who would bear the brunt of integration resisted it. They were often denounced as "racists" (even by fellow Jews), but in their own minds their motivation was concern for the education of their children and the maintenance of a Jewish community. This was one reason why the private, Jewish, all-day schools continued to grow. This was one way the Jew in the city avoided the impact of integration. (Yet we should point out that the number of such schools had been growing all through the fifties and sixties, when integration efforts had as yet made hardly any impact on the northern schools.)

Other issues led to conflicts between blacks and Jews and strained the liberal commitments of the Jewish community. In 1965 John Lindsay was elected mayor of New York City; he appointed, in response to black and Puerto Rican and liberal demands, a civilian board to investigate charges of police brutality. This was opposed by the police. They argued that their attempts to control crime would be hampered by such a board, and in 1966 they forced a referendum on whether the board should continue. The Jewish population in the city was severely split. While most Jewish organizations and the liberal-minded leaders of the Jewish community supported the board, the less prosperous Jews, in poorer areas where crime was severe, opposed it. Jews began to ask themselves for the first time whether they were still liberal.

Blacks demanded "community control" of the New York City schools in 1967. This meant that bodies elected by parents would control the schools. In New York, the majority of teachers were Jews and even more of the principals and supervisors. Teachers had achieved their positions through the merit system, the civil service, and they were protected by a powerful union. They feared this position would be undermined by community control, whose main immediate impact would be to replace Jewish teachers and principals by black ones. For this and other reasons they fought community control and engaged in a series of severe and damaging strikes in 1968–69 against it, which exacerbated relations between blacks and Jews. The Jewish community was split and Jews again wondered how liberal they were, after all. The split was clearly evident once again when Mayor Lindsay ran for re-election in 1969.

The significance of this for Judaism was that Judaism in America had been for a long time not much more than ethnic loyalty on the one hand and "liberalism" on the other. If anyone asked Jews what it meant to be a good Jew, as Marshall Sklare had done, the chief answers suggested simply support of the liberal view of the world—fairness, nondiscrimination, peace, good works. But the other side of the content of Judaism was ethnicity—support for Israel, for fellow Jews. The amalgam that was Judaism in the 1950's in America began to come apart in the 1960's, and after 1967 it came apart even faster. To be "liberal" in 1967 might mean to support Negro interests against Jewish interests, to support leftists who wished to see Israel destroyed, to oppose American aid to Israel. Liberalism and ethnic loyalty thus came into sharp collision. This perhaps was the chief significance of 1967. As it imposed on Jews a whole new view of the world, it required them to ask themselves, what is it to be Jewish, after all? If it is not to be liberal, what is it to be? Increasingly Jews chose the ethnic component in the disintegrating amalgam. And in response to 1967, ethnic loyalty became ever more paramount as the significant content of Judaism.

Jews still on the whole remained liberal, they still on the whole voted Democratic. But the steady strain between Israel and the left, on the one hand, and between Jewish interests in the United States and liberal and left positions, on the other, eroded the basis of the alliance between liberalism and ethnicity. One event will symbolize how far this erosion had gone. It had been for decades a central tenet of liberal faith in America that no public funds should go to support religious educational institutions. Indeed, this had been a source of tension between Jews and Catholics all through the 1950's and much of the 1960's. Almost every Jewish organization, religious and non-religious, supported the maintenance of the wall between church and state. When the Constitution of the state of New York was revised and put to the voters in 1968, it was voted down, largely because the new constitution weakened a stringent provision against public support for private (that is, religious) schools.

Only the Orthodox Jews supported public funds for private religious schools because, as I have pointed out, the largest number of Jewish day schools were Orthodox and the burden of supporting them with only privately raised funds was heavy. In November, 1971, for the first time the Synagogue Council of America, representing the rabbinical and congregational organizations of Conservative and Reform as well as Orthodox Jews, went on record supporting public funds for private religious schools. It is hard to think of any other action that could have so radically marked the split between liberalism and Judaism.

Inevitably, such developments further weakened those tendencies in Reform Judaism that emphasized social justice, a liberal stance, a universalistic point of view which played down the significance of Jews as a distinctive people. Inevitably, these developments encouraged a naïve and narrow-minded expression of Jewish self-interest in many quarters. One example of this was Rabbi Meir Kahane's Jewish Defense League, based in the poorer Orthodox sections of the Jewish community, which found a surprising response among some Jewish youth—surprising because the tactics of the JDL involved vigilante-like self-defense activities against crime in the older sections of the cities and offensive demonstrations against Soviet representatives on American soil. All this was anathema to liberal-minded Jews. But while official organizations denounced the JDL, many ordinary Jews gave them a sneaking or grudging admiration. Neither the movement nor this response would have been possible in the early 1960's. But in 1972 it expressed in a crude form the overwhelming insistence among so many Jews that Jewish interests were worthy and should be defended.

"Survival," which had for so long been criticized by Jewish religious thinkers and theologians as quite inadequate as a basis for Judaism and which had been regularly denounced as "*mere* survival," began to seem quite enough after 1967. Not perhaps enough for Judaism forever, but certainly enough for the moment. For without Jews, no further development of Judaism was possible, in any direction, whether that be simply the maintenance of the religious tradition, its adaptation to contemporary life, something in between, or something quite different. Survival was all-essential, and thus survival became a theological category.

And thus Jewish thinkers after 1967, and perhaps ordinary Jews, too, began to absorb the full meaning of Auschwitz, as they were recalled to consider it by the extraordinary days of June, 1967. The Jews had almost disappeared. That was Hitler's intention, and little enough stood in his way. Israel had almost disappeared. That was certainly the intention of the Arab leaders, and only Jewish strength stood in the way. In the light of these overwhelming facts, survival achieved a significance that made it quite impossible ever again to label it *"mere* survival."

Perhaps the most extreme consequences of this transformation of the idea of survival were drawn by Richard Rubenstein. Rubenstein emerged from Rabbi Mordecai Kaplan's Reconstructionist movement, and built on its emphasis on the importance of the Jewish people, aside from, indeed above, any body of fixed doctrine or fixed practice. He insisted that Auschwitz and Israel made quite irrelevant any supernatural view of the Jewish religion. God had not spoken at Auschwitz, or in 1967. So be it, he said. Survival demanded strength—and, as it appeared in Rubenstein's powerful article, "Homeland and Holocaust," nothing beyond that. "Whatever most diaspora Jews believe," he wrote, "they consider themselves primarily a distinctive religio-ethnic group rather than a community with a common creed. Far more Jews today accept the unity of Jewish destiny than the unity of Jewish belief." And further: "Of all the confusions experienced by the diaspora Jews, few

Epilogue

have been as great as the failure of many of their best religious minds to face the reality of modern Jewish history in both its agony and its triumph. Jewish history has written the final chapter in the terrible story of the God of history." (Rubenstein was the only Jewish theologian to be considered part of the "God is dead" movement of the 1960's. But he got to this position from a starting point very different from that of Christian theologians, from the experience of Auschwitz.)

When Arthur Cohen, criticizing him, wrote "What Rubenstein wants is force and potency, not faith and trust," Rubenstein agreed. But when Cohen asserted that this meant that Rubenstein had broken faith with the millions of Auschwitz, "who died with dignity and honor," Rubenstein forcefully disagreed. "I have attempted a diligent study of the Nazi extermination project, and I find myself aghast at the *indignity* of what took place. I am convinced that the wholly unanticipated character of the onslaught left Jews bereft of resources to counter the attack and to die fighting. . . . I am convinced my community's health demands that it face without illusion the full impact of its recent past."[10]

If Rubenstein had decided that Auschwitz and 1967 meant that Jews must never again trust anything but their own physical power—not other nations, not liberal good will and tolerance, not God—and most Jews, to a point, agreed, others still struggled with the old questions of what Judaism could mean in an age of horrors, fully experienced and barely avoided. Perhaps the most profound and impressive answers to these questions were those given by Emil L. Fackenheim. He did not dispense with the God of history, and he felt that a voice *had* spoken at Auschwitz, and in 1967, and it gave a clear command to Jews:

"What does the Voice of Auschwitz command?

" 'Jews are forbidden to hand Hitler posthumous victories. They are commanded to survive as Jews, lest the Jewish people perish. They are commanded to remember the victims of Auschwitz lest their memory perish. They are forbidden to despair of man and his world, and to escape into either cynicism or otherworldliness, lest they cooperate in delivering the world over to the forces of Auschwitz. Finally, they are forbidden to despair of the God of Israel, lest Judaism perish. A secularist Jew cannot make himself believe by a mere act of will, nor can he be commanded to do so. . . . And a religious Jew who has stayed with his God may be forced into new, possibly revolutionary relationships with Him. One possibility, however, is wholly unthinkable. A Jew may not respond to Hitler's attempt to destroy Judaism by himself cooperating in its destruction. In ancient times, the unthinkable Jewish sin was idolatry. Today, it is to respond to Hitler by doing his work.' "11

Thus, even for Fackenheim, for whom God still commanded, he commanded primarily—survival. The difference was, it would appear to me, though I am in no way a theologian, that for some it was enough, and others expected something more to come from it. For most Jews, quite ignorant of these controversies, the fact was that they *did* insist on remaining Jews, whatever that meant, or whatever it could mean. And that was the meaning of the Jewish response to 1967.

Appendix A

DECLARATION OF PRINCIPLES ADOPTED BY A GROUP OF REFORM RABBIS AT PITTSBURGH, 1885*

First—We recognize in every religion an attempt to grasp the Infinite One, and in every mode, source or book of revelation held sacred in any religious system the consciousness of the indwelling of God in man. We hold that Judaism presents the highest conception of the God-idea as taught in our holy Scriptures and developed and spiritualized by the Jewish teachers in accordance with the moral and philosophical progress of their respective ages. We maintain that Judaism preserved and defended amid continual struggles and trials and under enforced isolation this God-idea as the central religious truth for the human race.

Second—We recognize in the Bible the record of the consecration of the Jewish people to its mission as the priest of the One God, and value it as the most potent instrument of religious and moral instruction. We hold that the modern discoveries of scientific researches in the domains of nature and history are not antagonistic to the doctrines of Judaism, the Bible reflecting the primitive ideas of its own age and at times clothing its conception of divine providence and justice dealing with man in miraculous narratives.

Third—We recognize in the Mosaic legislation a system of training the Jewish people for its mission during its national life in Palestine, and today we accept as binding only its moral laws and maintain only such cere-monials as elevate and sanctify our lives, but reject all such as are not adapted to the views and habits of modern civilization.

Fourth—We hold that all such Mosaic and Rabbinical laws as regulate diet, priestly purity and dress originated in ages and under the influence of ideas altogether foreign to our present mental and spiritual state. They fail to impress the modern Jew with a spirit of priestly holiness; their ob-

* *Yearbook of the Central Conference of American Rabbis*, XLV (1935), 198–200.

servance in our day is apt rather to obstruct than to further modern spiritual elevation.

Fifth—We recognize in the modern era of universal culture of heart and intellect the approach of the realization of Israel's great Messianic hope for the establishment of the Kingdom of truth, justice and peace among all men. We consider ourselves no longer a nation but a religious community, and therefore expect neither a return to Palestine, nor a sacrificial worship under the administration of the sons of Aaron, nor the restoration of any of the laws concerning the Jewish state.

Sixth—We recognize in Judaism a progressive religion, ever striving to be in accord with the postulates of reason. We are convinced of the utmost necessity of preserving the historical identity with our great past. Christianity and Islam being daughter religions of Judaism, we appreciate their mission to aid in the spreading of monotheistic and moral truth. We acknowledge that the spirit of broad humanity of our age is our ally in the fulfilment of our mission, and therefore we extend the hand of fellowship to all who co-operate with us in the establishment of the reign of truth and righteousness among men.

Seventh—We reassert the doctrine of Judaism, that the soul of man is immortal, grounding this belief on the divine nature of the human spirit, which forever finds bliss in righteousness and misery in wickedness. We reject as ideas not rooted in Judaism the belief both in bodily resurrection and in Gehenna and Eden (hell and paradise), as abodes for everlasting punishment or reward.

Eighth—In full accordance with the spirit of Mosaic legislation which strives to regulate the relation between rich and poor, we deem it our duty to participate in the great task of modern times, to solve on the basis of justice and righteousness the problems presented by the contrasts and evils of the present organization of society.

Notes

CHAPTER I

1. The best guidance to this complicated field is to be found in the annual volumes of the *American Jewish Year Book*, which publishes analytical articles, summaries of surveys of Jewish population, and estimates of Jewish population by state and community. For the most recent authoritative article, see Sidney Goldstein, "American Jewry, 1970: A Demographic Profile," *American Jewish Year Book*, 1971.

CHAPTER II

1. David and Tamar de Sola Pool, *An Old Faith in the New World* (New York, 1955), p. 227.

CHAPTER III

1. David Philipson and Louis Grossman, *Selected Writings of Isaac Mayer Wise* (Cincinnati, 1900), p. 40. (Reprinted from the *Occident*, December, 1848.)

2. Barnett A. Elzas, *The Jews of South Carolina* (Philadelphia, 1905), p. 160.

3. Allen Tarshish, "The Rise of American Judaism" (unpublished thesis in the library of Hebrew Union College, 1938), p. xv.

4. *Ibid.*, pp. i–xiii.

5. Benno M. Wallach, "Dr. David Einhorn's Sinai" (unpublished thesis in the library of Hebrew Union College, 1950), p. 197.

6. David Philipson, *The Reform Movement in Modern Judaism* (New York, 1931), pp. 355–57.

CHAPTER IV

1. Jacob Rader Marcus (ed.), *Memoirs of American Jews, 1775–1865* (Philadelphia, 1955), II, 83.

2. Richard Gottheil, *The Life of Gustav Gottheil* (Williamsport, Pa., 1936), pp. 182, 232.

3. J. L. Magnes, *Reformed Judaism—Plans for Reconstruction*, sermon preached April 24, 1910 (pamphlet), p. 13.

4. David Philipson, *The Reform Movement in Modern Judaism* (New York, 1931), p. 349.

5. Beryl Harold Levy, *Reform Judaism in America* (New York, 1933), p. 3.

6. *Ibid.*

7. Joshua Trachtenberg, *Consider the Years* (Easton, Pa., 1944), pp. 182–83.

8. *Yearbook of the Central Conference of American Rabbis*, XIX (1909), 170.

9. Kaufmann Kohler, *Jewish Theology* (New York, 1928), pp. 445–46.

10. David Philipson, *My Life as an American Jew* (Cincinnati, 1941), p. 23.

11. *Jewish Theological Seminary Students Annual* (New York, 1914), p. 17.

12. Herbert Parzen, "The Early Development of Conservative Judaism," *Conservative Judaism*, III (1947), 15.

CHAPTER V

1. Irving Aaron Mandel, "The Attitude of the American Jewish Community toward East European Immigration as Reflected in the Anglo-Jewish Press (1880–1890)," *American Jewish Archives*, VII (1950), 24.

2. *Ibid.*, p. 25.

3. Jacob I. Hartstein, in *American Jewish Year Book*, 1946–47, p. 75.

4. Herbert Parzen, "The Early Development of Conservative Judaism," *Conservative Judaism*, III (1947), 16.

CHAPTER VI

1. *Report of the U.S. Industrial Commission* (Washington, 1901), XV, 325–27.

2. *Ibid.*, p. 478.

Notes

3. Mordecai Kaplan, *Judaism as a Civilization* (New York, 1934), pp. 78–79.

4. *Ibid.*, p. 328.

5. *Ibid.*, p. 184.

6. *Yearbook of the Central Conference of American Rabbis*, V (1894), 69.

7. *Ibid.*, VIII (1897), xii.

8. *Ibid.*, XLVII (1937), 97–98.

CHAPTER VII

1. From a study by Arthur Hertzberg which is to appear in a volume of essays in honor of Salo Baron.

2. Marshall Sklare, Marc Vosk, and Mark Zborowski, "Forms and Expressions of Jewish Identification," *Jewish Social Studies*, XVII (1955), 209.

3. Jerome F. Molino, "The Rabbi's Personal Religion," *CCAR Journal*, April, 1954, p. 20.

4. Alexander S. Kline, "The Rabbi in the Small Town," *CCAR Journal*, April, 1954, pp. 10–11.

5. "Secularism in a Religious Framework," *Judaism*, I (1952), 36–43.

CHAPTER VIII

1. Public Opinion News Service release, December 18, 1954.

2. *Proceedings of the Rabbinical Assembly of America*, IV (1932), 358.

CHAPTER IX

1. Jakob J. Petuchowski, *Heirs of the Pharisees* (New York: Basic Books, 1970), pp. 189–90.

2. Erich Rosenthal, "Studies of Jewish Intermarriage in the United States," and "Jewish Intermarriage in Indiana," *American Jewish Year Book*, 1963 and 1968.

3. See note 1, chapter 1.

4. Petuchowski, pp. 184–85, first published in *The Reconstructionist* in 1960.

5. Jacob Neusner, *Fellowship in Judaism: The First Century and Today* (London: Valentine, Mitchell, 1963), pp. 73–74.

6. *American Jewish Year Book*, 1968, p. 278.

7. *Ibid.*, pp. 69 and 210.

8. Donald R. Cutler (ed.), *The Religious Situation: 1968* (Boston: Beacon Press, 1968), p. 44.

9. George E. Gruen, "Aspects and Prospects of the Interaction between American Jews and Israel," *Conference on American Jewish Dilemmas, 1971*, American Federation of Jews from Central Europe, 1971.

10. Cutler, pp. 41, 61, 102, 103.

11. Emil L. Fackenheim, *God's Presence in History* (New York: New York University Press, 1970), p. 84, where Fackenheim quotes his own 1967 article in *Commentary*, "Jewish Faith and the Holocaust."

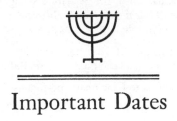

Important Dates

1492   The Jews are expelled from Spain; Columbus discovers America, and the first Jew steps on American soil

1630–54   A large Jewish community exists in Recife, Brazil

1654   Refugees from this community land in New Amsterdam to found the first Jewish community on the territory that is now the United States

1677   A second Jewish community exists in Newport, Rhode Island

1730's and 1740's   Jewish congregations are established in Savannah, Georgia; Philadelphia, Pennsylvania; and Charleston, South Carolina

1749   The last date for the use of Portuguese in the official records of Shearith Israel, synagogue of the Jewish community in New York

1763   The synagogue of Newport, Rhode Island, is dedicated—the only surviving synagogue building of the eighteenth century

1802   The first synagogue following the Ashkenazic rite is established in Philadelphia

1824   The Reformed Society of Israelites is organized in Charleston

1836   The first mass movement of Jews to the United States begins in Bavaria

1840   Abraham Rice, the first rabbi to come to America, takes office in Baltimore

1841–57   Leo Merzbacher, Max Lilienthal, Isaac Mayer Wise, Bernhard Felsenthal, David Einhorn, Samuel Adler, and other German rabbis come to America to serve the new German congregations, and are active in promoting reforms in Judaism

American Judaism

1843   Isaac Leeser, hazzan of the Sephardic synagogue of Philadelphia, founds the *Occident and Jewish Advocate*, a strong supporter of conservatism in religion

1852   The first synagogue of East European Jews is founded in New York City (one had been established in Buffalo as early as 1848)

1854   I. M. Wise moves to Cincinnati and founds the *Israelite*

1857   Wise publishes his radically revised prayer book in Hebrew and German

1860   Morris Raphall becomes the first rabbi to open a session of the United States Congress with prayer
The religious census reports seventy-seven Jewish synagogues

1864   Maimonides College is established in Philadelphia (it closed in 1873)
Benjamin Szold of Baltimore (arrived 1859) publishes his prayer book, which is somewhat more conservative than Wise's

1866   Samuel Hirsch and Marcus Jastrow, two leading German scholar-rabbis, arrive to take pulpits in Philadelphia

1869   A group of Reform rabbis under the leadership of Hirsch and Einhorn meets in Philadelphia to publish the first statement of the Reform position in America

1870   The religious census reports 189 congregations, 152 synagogue buildings

1873   Wise founds the Union of American Hebrew Congregations; Felix Adler breaks with Reform Judaism, to found (in |1876) the Ethical Culture movement

1875   Wise founds Hebrew Union College

1875–78   A survey of the Union of American Hebrew Congregations reports there are 270 congregations and 230,000 Jews in the United States

1881   The mass movement of East European Jews to America begins, sparked by the pogroms of 1881 and the Russian decrees of 1882

1883   The first class of Hebrew Union College is graduated, and the conservative element is shocked by the violation of the laws of *kashrut*

Important Dates

1885   The Reform rabbis meet in Pittsburgh to adopt a statement of principles

1886   In answer to the Pittsburgh meeting, Sabato Morais of the Sephardic synagogue of Philadelphia, H. Pereira Mendes of the Sephardic synagogue of New York, and other conservatives found the Jewish Theological Seminary Association, which begins to conduct classes in 1887

1888   Jacob Joseph arrives in New York to serve as chief rabbi for a group of East European Orthodox synagogues

1889   The Central Conference of American Rabbis (Isaac Mayer Wise, president) is founded

1890   The religious census reports 533 congregations, 301 synagogue buildings

1894   The Union Prayer Book is published by the Central Conference of American Rabbis

1896   The first American yeshiva (Rabbi Isaac Elchanan Theological Seminary)—school for higher education in the East European system of Jewish education—is founded

1897   The first Zionist Congress meets in Basel; the Central Conference of American Rabbis, under Isaac Mayer Wise's urging, unanimously condemns Zionism

1898   The Union of Orthodox Jewish Congregations is founded by the conservative elements and captured by the immigrant East European Orthodox elements

1900   Death of Isaac Mayer Wise

1902   East European Orthodox rabbis found the Union of Orthodox Rabbis
A reorganized Jewish Theological Seminary begins operations under the presidency of Solomon Schechter

1903   Kaufmann Kohler becomes president of Hebrew Union College

1905   *The Jewish Encyclopedia* is published; it estimates there are 1,700,-000 Jews in the United States

1906   The religious census reports there are 1,769 congregations and 821
        synagogue buildings
        The American Jewish Committee is founded in response to the
        Kishinev pogrom
        Stephen S. Wise insists, in an exchange of letters with Temple
        Emanuel, on the right to advocate his personal views from the
        pulpit; he is refused the pulpit and founds his own Free Syna-
        gogue

1907   Three members of the faculty of Hebrew Union College resign
        because of their Zionist sentiments

1909   Gifts from Jacob L. Schiff lead to the establishment of Jewish
        teachers' training programs at the Jewish Theological Seminary
        and Hebrew Union College

1910   Judah L. Magnes attacks Reform Judaism for its emptiness, from
        the pulpit of Temple Emanuel
        The first Yiddish secular school system is begun by the socialist
        Zionist group

1913   Solomon Schechter founds the United Synagogue of America (Con-
        servative)

1915   Solomon Schechter dies; Cyrus Adler succeeds him as president of
        the Jewish Theological Seminary and the United Synagogue of
        America
        Rabbi Isaac Elchanan Theological Seminary and Yeshiva Etz
        Chaim (an Orthodox secondary school) are united under Bernard
        Revel

1916   The religious census reports there are 1,901 congregations and 866
        synagogue buildings

1917   The *American Jewish Year Book* estimates there are 3,300,000 Jews
        in the United States
        An official Jewish translation of the Hebrew Bible is published by
        the Jewish Publication Society of America
        The Balfour Declaration is greeted by American Zionists; Zionism
        becomes a great mass movement in American Jewish life but is
        somewhat deflated at the end of the war

1918   The Jewish Center (a synagogue-center) is founded by Mordecai
        Kaplan in New York City

Important Dates

1919   The Rabbinical Assembly of America is founded as the central body of Conservative rabbis

1921   Kaufmann Kohler is succeeded as president of Hebrew Union College by Julian Morgenstern

1922   Stephen S. Wise founds the Jewish Institute of Religion, training rabbis (mostly for the Reform group) with a more national orientation than that given by Hebrew Union College
A permanent American Jewish Congress, representing the Zionist-minded, East European element, is founded

1924   This is the last year of heavy East European immigration before strict quotas are imposed

1926   The religious census reports 3,118 congregations and 1,782 synagogue buildings, and the Jewish population of the United States is estimated at 4,100,000

1928   The Rabbi Isaac Elchanan Yeshiva grows into Yeshiva College, first general institution of higher education under Jewish auspices

1930   At the annual meeting of the (Conservative) Rabbinical Assembly, Rabbi Louis Epstein proposes a solution to the problem of the *agunah*—the woman whose husband is presumed dead but who, by Jewish religious law, cannot marry unless there are witnesses to his death

1933   Hitler takes power; the persecution and emigration of German Jews begins; Stephen S. Wise leads the Jewish boycott of German goods

1934   The United Jewish Appeal, raising money for European Jews, refugees, and Palestine, launches its first campaign
Judaism as a Civilization, by Mordecai Kaplan, is published

1935   The *Reconstructionist* magazine is started to express Kaplan's ideas
The Rabbinical Council of America, an organization of the English-speaking Orthodox rabbis, is formed

1936   The religious census reports 3,738 congregations and 2,851 synagogue buildings; and the Jewish population is estimated at 4,600,000

1937   The Central Conference of American Rabbis adopts a new statement of principles, more traditional and national than the Pittsburgh statement of 1885

1938   The United Yeshivos Foundation is founded to help support all-day Orthodox schools

1939   The British White Paper on Palestine is issued, and immigration to that country is reduced to a trickle; the European war begins, and the first news of the slaughter of the Polish Jews reaches America

1940   Bernard Revel, president of Yeshiva College, dies
Cyrus Adler dies; Louis Finkelstein succeeds him as president of the Jewish Theological Seminary
A revised Union Prayer Book—a shade more traditional than the Union Prayer Book of 1894—is issued by the Reform rabbinate
The Lubavitcher *rebbe*, leader of the Habad Hasidim, arrives in America, a refugee from Hitler, and immediately begins work establishing all-day schools for Jewish children

1942   The Zionist movement, strengthened in America by the disaster in Europe and British intransigence in Palestine, adopts the Biltmore platform, calling for a Jewish state in Palestine. A small minority of Reform rabbis attacks the Zionist platform; an overwhelming majority defends it. Some anti-Zionist Reform rabbis and anti-Zionist laymen organize the American Council for Judaism, the only organization in American Jewish life that upholds the position that the Jews are only a religious group and in no way a national group

1943   The Central Conference of American Rabbis adopts a resolution agreeing that both the Zionist and anti-Zionist positions are compatible with Reform Judaism
Samuel Belkin becomes president of Yeshiva College

1944   American Jews become aware of the full dimensions of the European tragedy

1945   The Reconstructionist Foundation issues a new, revised prayer book, much less radical than the standard Reform prayer book; the Union of Orthodox Rabbis takes the occasion to excommunicate Mordecai Kaplan; the excommunication—attacked by the

Reform and Conservative rabbinate—emphasizes the crisis in Jewish law

Yeshiva College becomes Yeshiva University

1946 The Conservative rabbinate issues its first uniform prayer book—it is hardly distinguishable from the traditional prayer book

1947 Nelson Glueck becomes president of Hebrew Union College

1948 The British withdraw from Palestine; the Jewish state is declared; and Israel successfully defends itself against Arab attack

The Conservative rabbinate conducts an inconclusive conference on Jewish law

Brandeis University, a secular college under Jewish auspices, opens

Synagogue-building on a large scale goes on throughout the country

1949 Hebrew Union College and the Jewish Institute of Religion merge

1951 The publication of Will Herberg's *Judaism for Modern Man* and Abraham Joshua Heschel's *Man Is Not Alone* are only two signs of a growing interest in Jewish theology and Jewish religious thought

1954 After twenty-four years of discussion, the Rabbinical Assembly adopts a new marriage contract to solve the problem of the *agunah* and other problems raised by Jewish marriage law; this action is violently attacked by the Orthodox rabbinate, which refuses to accept the authority of the Conservative rabbinate to make changes in Jewish law

1956 Statistics in the *American Jewish Year Book* show a great increase in Jewish synagogue membership in the previous fifteen years, particularly in the Reform and Conservative groups, and a great increase in Jewish religious school attendance

1961 The trial of Adolf Eichmann in Jerusalem encourages deeper consideration of the Holocaust and its meaning for Jews and Judaism

1962–63 The expansion in synagogues, memberships, and school enrolments reaches a plateau, except for Orthodox day schools which continue to expand

1965   The Vatican Council, after four years of deliberation, be-
       hind the scenes and in public, adopts a declaration on the
       relation of the Church to the Jews which asserts that "what
       happened in His Passion cannot be charged against all
       Jews, then alive, nor against Jews of today," and that
       "mindful of the patrimony she shares with the Jews, [the
       Church] . . . decries hatred, persecution, displays of anti-
       Semitism, directed against Jews at any time and by any-
       one." Reform Jews welcome the growing movement
       toward inter-religious dialogue, Conservatives welcome it
       more cautiously, Orthodox reject it

1967   The six-day war produces an unexpected and overwhelming
       reaction among American Jews: an unparalleled outpour-
       ing of money, and a deepened sense of Jewish identity and
       of participation in a common Jewish fate
       The strong alliance between young Jews and the New Left
       is shaken by the opposition of certain New Left elements
       to Israel
       Black militancy, expressed in separatism and occasionally in
       anti-Zionism and anti-Semitism, leads to a strain in the
       sympathy of Jewish liberals and radicals for blacks
       One expression of young Jews to find a more meaningful
       Jewishness is the founding of the magazine *Response*
       The Boston *havurah* (a "fellowship" devoted to study, and a
       search for community) is founded by young Jews, and the
       New York *havurah* follows a year later
       Jewish religious figures angrily criticize Christian spokesmen
       for failing to support Israel strongly, before and after the
       war. The Christian-Jewish dialogue is badly damaged

1968   Jewish-black relations are further damaged by the fierce New
       York teachers' strike of 1968, in which unionized teachers,
       mainly Jewish, confront black groups demanding commu-
       nity control
       In the year after the 1967 war, an exceptional number of
       serious works in Jewish theology by North American writ-
       ers is published: *Quest for Past and Future: Essays in Jew-
       ish Theology*, by Emil L. Fackenheim; *Ever Since Sinai*,

by Jakob L. Petuchowski; *The Religious Imagination*, by Richard L. Rubenstein; *New Jewish Theology in the Making*, by Eugene B. Borowitz. Rubenstein's article, "Homeland and Holocaust," in *The Religious Situation, 1968*, edited by Donald R. Cutler, with commentaries by Milton Himmelfarb, Zalman M. Schachter, Arthur A. Cohen, and Irving Greenberg, emphasizes the growing importance of the Holocaust for Jewish religious thinking

1969   *The Jewish Radical*, the first of what are to become a flood of Jewish student newspapers combining radical criticism of American society and the Jewish "establishment" with a strong positive attitude toward Jewish tradition, Israel, and Soviet Jews, is founded in Berkeley. In spring 1971, it is estimated there are 36 such newspapers

1970   The publication of serious American Jewish theology continues with Jakob J. Petuchowski, *The Heirs of the Pharisees;* Jacob Neusner, *Judaism in the Secular Age;* and Emil L. Fackenheim, *God's Presence in History*

      Sh'ma, a biweekly edited by Rabbi Eugene B. Borowitz, is founded, and expresses the new concerns of many young rabbis—for a new spirit of community, for a new involvement of Judaism with current political and moral issues, for an "interdenominational" Judaism overcoming the conflicts of institutional Judaism

1971   The Synagogue Council of America, representing all three major branches of American Judaism, for the first time comes out in favor of public support to private religious schools, a significant break with one major tenet of American liberalism to which Jews had adhered, the separation of church and state

Suggested Reading

This is by no means a complete bibliography. It lists the major works in the field, and some others which have been particularly useful to me and on which I have drawn heavily. Its purpose is twofold—to direct the interested reader to other works on American Judaism and to acknowledge my indebtedness to the works and writers listed. Many books and articles are relevant for more than one chapter: in that case, they are listed under the chapter for which they have been most useful.

GENERAL WORKS

Invaluable for the study of any subject in American Jewish history is Moses Rischin's *An Inventory of American Jewish History* (Cambridge, Mass., 1954). It surveys the source materials for American Jewish history and lists almost every work of any value. "Jewish Religious Life and Institutions in America: An Historical Study," by Moshe Davis, in *The Jews: Their History, Culture, and Religion*, ed. Louis Finkelstein (New York, 1949), pp. 354–453, is an extremely detailed and useful history of Judaism in America and contains material to be found nowhere else. Jewish religious statistics were gathered by the United States Census, or official census agents, at ten-year intervals between 1850 and 1890 and between 1906 and 1936. All this information has been summarized by Uriah Zevi Engelman in "Jewish Statistics in the U.S. Census of Religious Bodies (1850–1936)," *Jewish Social Studies*, IX (1947), 127–74. For the social and economic background of American Jewish history, see Nathan Glazer's "Social Characteristics of American Jews, 1654–1954," *American Jewish Year Book*, LVI (1955), 3–41.

CHAPTER II

The most valuable works for this period are Jacob Rader Marcus, *Early American Jewry* (3 vols.; Philadelphia, 1951, 1953); Hyman B. Grinstein, *The Rise of the Jewish Community of New York, 1654–1860* (Philadelphia,

Suggested Reading

1947); and David and Tamar de Sola Pool, *An Old Faith in the New World* (New York, 1955). On the background of the first Jewish settlement in New Amsterdam, see I. S. Emmanuel, "New Light on Early American Jewry," *American Jewish Archives*, VII (1955), 3–64, and Arnold Wiznitzer, *The Records of the Earliest Jewish Community in the New World* (New York, 1954).

CHAPTER III

On the German Jewish immigration and its background, I have found most useful two articles by Rudolph Glanz, "The Immigration of German Jews up to 1880," *Yivo Annual of Jewish Social Science*, II–III (1947–48), 81–99, and "Source Materials on the History of Jewish Immigration to the United States, 1800–1880," *ibid.*, VI (1951), 73–156. On the Reform movement, its German background and American history, the standard work is David Philipson's *The Reform Movement in Judaism* (New York, 1931). There are a number of able theses on the Reform movement in the library of Hebrew Union College, of which the following have been particularly helpful: Wolfgang Kaelter, "Liberal Judaism in Germany" (1950); Benno M. Wallach, "David Einhorn's Sinai" (1950); Martin B. Ryback, "The East-West Conflict in American Reform, 1854–79" (summarized in an article in *American Jewish Archives*, IV [1952], 3–25); Jerome W. Grollman, "The Emergence of Reform Judaism in the United States" (summarized in an article in *American Jewish Archives*, II [1950], 3–14); Robert I. Kahn, "Liberalism as Reflected in Jewish Preaching in the English Language in the Mid-19th Century" (1951); Allan Tarshish, "The Rise of American Judaism" (1938).

There is a good deal of autobiographical material of value relating to this period: see the excellent collection by Jacob Rader Marcus, *Memoirs of American Jews, 1775–1865* (2 vols.; Philadelphia, 1955). The writings of Isaac Mayer Wise, *Reminiscences* (New York, 1935) and *Selected Writings*, ed. David Philipson and Louis Grossman (Cincinnati, 1900), are vivid and indispensable. There are biographies of other immigrant German rabbis of this period: *Max Lilienthal*, by David Philipson (New York, 1915); *Bernhard Felsenthal*, by Emma Felsenthal (New York, 1944); and *Moses Mielziner*, by Ella M. Mielziner (New York, 1931). Many congregational histories have detailed accounts of the progress of reform. See, for example, *The History of Oheb Shalom, 1853–1953*, by Louis F. Cahn (Baltimore, 1953); *As Yesterday When It Is Past*, by James G. Heller (Cincinnati, 1952), the history of Isaac M. Wise's synagogue in Cincinnati. There is an excellent account of the Reform movement in Charleston, South Carolina, in Barnett A. Elzas' *The Jews of South Carolina* (Philadelphia, 1905).

CHAPTER IV

An invaluable work for the theology and ideology of the Reform movement is Beryl Harold Levy's *Reform Judaism in America* (New York, 1933). Julius Morgenstern's *As a Mighty Stream* (Philadelphia, 1949) contains interesting essays on "classic Reform" (as the Reform movement of this period is called) and its problems. *Growth and Achievement: Temple Israel, 1854–1954*, ed. Arthur Mann, has excellent essays on Rabbis Schindler and Fleischer. Other valuable congregational histories are Israel Goldstein, *A Century of Judaism in New York* (1930) (B'nai Jeshurun); Joshua Trachtenberg, *Consider the Years: The Story of the Jewish Community of Easton, Pennsylvania, 1752–1942* (Easton, Pa., 1944); Simon Cohen, *Shaaray Tefila: A History of Its Hundred Years, 1845–1945* (New York, 1945); and (no author) *The Temple, 1850–1950* (Cleveland, 1950). There are biographies of *Solomon Schechter*, by Norman Bentwich (Philadelphia, 1938); "Cyrus Adler," by A. A. Neumann, *American Jewish Year Book*, Vol. XLII (1940); *Jacob Schiff*, by Cyrus Adler (New York, 1928); Judah L. Magnes (*For Zion's Sake*), by Norman Bentwich (Philadelphia, 1954); *Gustav Gottheil*, by Richard Gottheil (Williamsport, Pa., 1936). There are useful autobiographies by David Philipson, *My Life as an American Jew* (Cincinnati, 1941), and Cyrus Adler, *I Have Considered the Years* (Philadelphia, 1941). The Reform movement has done an excellent job of documenting itself in the *Yearbook of the Central Conference of American Rabbis* (beginning in 1890) and the *Proceedings of the Union of American Hebrew Congregations* (beginning in 1873). Moshe Davis, *The Emergence of Conservative Judaism* (Philadelphia, 1963), is a detailed study of this period.

CHAPTER V

A good background work on the Jews of eastern Europe is S. M. Dubnow's *History of the Jews in Russia and Poland* (3 vols.; Philadelphia, 1916–20). The most valuable book on East European immigration is the two-volume, uncompleted *History of the Jewish Labor Movement in the United States* (in Yiddish), ed. E. Tcherikover (New York, 1943, 1945). Sections of this work have been translated into English and may be found scattered through the volumes of the *Yivo Annual of Jewish Social Science*, which also

Suggested Reading

contains other valuable articles on East European Jews in America. A shorter work is Melech Epstein's *Jewish Labor in USA, 1882–1914* (New York, 1950). Basic materials for this period are to be found in the reports of the U.S. Industrial Commission, 1901, and the U.S. Immigration Commission, 1910. There is a useful account of German Jewish reaction to East European immigration by Irving Aaron Mandel in *American Jewish Archives*, III (1950), 8–36. On the religious life of the East European Jews in America, there is no good account. Novels are revealing for this (and subsequent) periods. Oblique light is thrown on the religious situation by the *Jewish Communal Register of New York City, 1917–18*; Alexander M. Dushkin's *Jewish Education in New York City* (New York, 1917); and the volumes of the *American Jewish Year Book*, from 1899 to the present. For the story of Jacob Joseph see Abraham J. Karp, "New York Chooses a Chief Rabbi," *Publications of the American Jewish Historical Society*, XLIV (1955), 129–98.

CHAPTER VI

For this period, too, as much, or more, may be learned from novels as from any other written source. See, for example, Meyer Levin's *The Old Bunch* and Ann Birstein's *Star of Glass*. *Commentary on the American Scene*, ed. Elliot E. Cohen (New York, 1953), contains a valuable collection of essays dealing with the Jewish life of this period. For a general treatment of the movement from the ghetto to the areas of second settlement, see Louis Wirth's *The Ghetto* (Chicago, 1928, reprinted 1956). On Yiddish school systems, see S. Yefroikin, "Yiddish Secular Schools in the United States," *The Jewish People*, II (New York, 1948), 144–50. On religious attitudes of Jewish youth, see Nathan Goldberg's "Religious and Social Attitudes of Jewish Youth in the U.S.A.," *Jewish Review*, I (1943), 135–68, and Nettie Pauline McGill's "Some Characteristics of Jewish Youth in New York City," *Jewish Social Service Quarterly*, XIV (1938), 251–72. For Horace Kallen's point of view, see his collections of essays, *Culture and Democracy in the United States* (New York, 1924) and *Judaism at Bay* (New York, 1932). For Mordecai Kaplan's point of view, see *Judaism as a Civilization* (New York, 1934), and *Mordecai Kaplan: An Evaluation*, ed. Ira Eisenstein and Eugene Kohn (New York, 1952). For the history of the Jewish Center, see *The JWB Survey*, by Oscar Janowsky (New York, 1948). For the history of Conservatism, there is an excellent study by Marshall Sklare, *Conservative Judaism* (Glencoe, Ill., 1955), and good studies by Herbert Parzen in *Conservative Judaism*, III–VII (1947–50). *The Jewish Theological*

Seminary of America, Semi-centennial Volume, ed. Cyrus Adler (New York, 1939), is useful for the history of that institution. The *Proceedings of the Rabbinical Assembly of America* (1930 on, with one earlier volume for 1927) and the *Reports of the United Synagogue of America* (from 1913 to the early twenties—there is one volume of *Proceedings* for 1950) are less complete and less accessible than the parallel series for the Reform group. The story of Reform Judaism in Sioux City is taken from the thesis of Martin Hinchin, "A History of the Jews of Sioux City, Iowa, 1857–1945," (Hebrew Union College, 1946). *Reform Judaism* (Cincinnati, 1949), a collection of essays, is valuable for the developments in Reform Judaism, 1920–40. The series of *Proceedings of the UAHC* and *Yearbook of the CCAR* are, of course, the basic source.

CHAPTER VII

Most of this chapter is based on personal observation. The volumes of the *American Jewish Year Book* have been particularly valuable for their annual reports on religion, beginning with Vol. XLIV (1943), covering the years 1941–42. Will Herberg's *Protestant, Catholic, Jew* (New York, 1955) is a stimulating account of the religious revival and comes to conclusions very similar to those drawn in this chapter. Herbert Gans's study of the Jewish community of Park Forest—a short version of which appeared in *Commentary,* XI (1951), 330–39—has contributed a good deal to my thinking on this subject, as has Marshall Sklare's book on Conservative Judaism. Harry Gersh's "The New Suburbanites of the 50's," *Commentary,* XVII (1954), 209–21, is a good essay on the move to the suburbs. The facts on Jewish education in the New York region are from surveys reported in the *JEC* [Jewish Education Committee] *Bulletin.*

Of the material on Jewish religious practice, identity, and institutions that has become available since 1956, the most valuable is: Marshall Sklare and Joseph Greenblum, *Jewish Identity on the Suburban Frontier* (New York, 1967); Sidney Goldstein and Calvin Goldscheider, *Jewish-Americans: Three Generations in a Jewish Community* (Englewood Cliffs, N.J., 1968); articles by Charles S. Liebman on Orthodoxy, theological seminaries, and Reconstruction, in the *American Jewish Year Book* for the years 1965, 1968, and 1971; and an article on Jewish education by Walter I. Ackerman, in the *American Jewish Year Book, 1969.*

Suggested Reading

CHAPTER VIII

On the political behavior of American Jews, see Lawrence Fuchs, *Political Behavior of American Jews* (Glencoe, Illinois, 1956). For further discussion of the problem of Jewish liberalism and radicalism, see Nathan Glazer, *The Social Basis of American Communism* (New York, 1961), chap. 4; and Charles S. Liebman, "Toward a Theory of Jewish Liberalism," in Donald R. Cutler, *The Religious Situation, 1968* (Boston, 1968), pp. 1034–61. Good analyses of Jewish political behavior are to be found in the annual volumes of the *American Jewish Year Book* by Lucy S. Dawidowicz and others (see, for example, *1967*, pp. 88–91), in Milton Himmelfarb, "Are Jews Still Liberal?" *Commentary*, XLIII (1967), 67–72, and in articles by Himmelfarb in subsequent issues of *Commentary*. The section on the Hasidic revival in Williamsburg is based on George Kranzler, *Williamsburg: A Jewish Community in Transition* (New York, 1961). Since this section was written two other books have appeared: Solomon Poll, *The Hasidic Community of Williamsburg* (New York, 1967), and the impressive and scholarly work of Jerome R. Mintz, *Legends of the Hasidim* (Chicago, 1968).

Index

Index